MEN, WOMEN, & GOD

families today and tomorrow

by David and Vera Mace

JOHN KNOX PRESS
ATLANTA

Library of Congress Cataloging in Publication Data

Mace, David.
   Men, women, and God.

    1. Family—Religious life. 2. Family life education.
I. Mace, Vera, joint author. II. Title.
BV4526.2.M24   248'.4   76–7225
ISBN 0–8042–9076–2

Third printing 1978

Printed in the United States of America

Preface

IN OFFERING OUR BOOK to its readers, we need to provide a few words of explanation.

First the title is not original. In 1923 a book was published in England by the Student Christian Movement Press, entitled *Men, Women, and God*, and a number of editions appeared before it finally went out of print. The author of the book was Dr. A. Herbert Gray, a distinguished Scottish Presbyterian minister with whom we were later (between 1942 and 1949) closely associated in the establishment in Britain of the National Marriage Guidance Council, of which he was president and we were executive directors. We have used his title for our book not only because it conveniently describes what we want to discuss, but also as a token of our deep affection and respect for him, and as a tribute to his pioneering work in exploring the Christian understanding of the man-woman relationship.

Second, we have adopted an unusual approach: our book is based on a program carried out in First Presbyterian Church of Setonville, Ohio. The place and all the characters who take part are of course fictitious. But it seemed to us that this way of writing up our material would make it more interesting to the reader. In addition, since the book has been also planned as a resource for group study, this approach enables us to present subjects in a manner that quickly raises controversial questions, which should lead to lively discussions.

Third, we should make it clear that the attitudes and viewpoints of the various speakers are not necessarily our own. We wanted a wide variety of opinions to be expressed, and obviously these cannot always be reconciled. We should explain also that we submitted the manuscript to an editorial committee which represented a number of different church groups. We decided to accept all the changes they suggested whether we agreed with them or not. So the book, beyond the work we did in preparing it, represents some hard work on the part of quite a number of people.

So we offer the book to its readers in the hope that, if it doesn't come up with all the answers, it may at least raise some of the more important questions which Christians must face today as they think about men, women, and God.

David and Vera Mace

Contents

Introduction

Item from Church Bulletin
First Presbyterian Church, Setonville, Ohio

STARTING WEDNESDAY EVENING, March 12, we're going to look
at some answers to these troublesome questions. Each Wednesday, from 8:00 to 10:00, our pastor, with the help of family life
specialists in our community, will be leading a discussion in the
Fellowship Hall on "Men, Women, and God: Families Today and
Tomorrow." The series is open to everyone free of charge, and
runs for twelve weeks.

Many Christians are confused about the whole area of man-
woman relationships. We hear disturbing reports about broken
marriages . . . people living together outside of marriage . . .
communal living . . . the extended family . . . cloning and test-
tube babies. Voices cry out that the whole institution of the family
is hopelessly anachronistic. Dire predictions are made that traditional family styles are doomed, that children will no longer be
raised by parents, that babies will be born without women having
to go through the ordeal of pregnancy and childbirth.

The officers of our church feel it is time for us to think through
these issues. What do we as Christians really believe about sex,
marriage, parenthood, and family life? We need to clarify our
thinking before we can stand for our convictions.

Each session begins with speakers who discuss a selected subject from varying viewpoints. Time will be allowed for questions
and answers. Before 9:00 P.M. participants will go into discussion
groups of approximately twelve people each to share concerns and

insights, and the leaders for that evening will be available to these groups.

We believe this will be a profitable experience for us here at First Presbyterian Church. Make plans to join us for the entire twelve sessions, and bring your friends.

Chapter 1

The Family

THE DOWNSTAIRS AUDITORIUM of the First Presbyterian Church is full as Pastor Jack Russell motions Professor Arthur Jones to precede him to the platform. The pastor goes to the speaker's stand and the buzz of conversation dies away.

"I'm delighted," he says, "that you have turned out in such good numbers for the first session of our series on 'Men, Women, and God: Families Today and Tomorrow.'

"Let me tell you what the steering committee has planned for this evening. First, our guest speaker will briefly summarize some sociological insights about the family, its nature and functions. Then I'll say something about our Christian teaching on the subject. After that, Dr. Jones and I will answer questions from the floor. Then we'll go into small groups for about forty minutes of discussion. We won't try to come back together again, so each group will stop when it wants to. And rather than having a service of worship here, we're asking each small group to plan to take time for worship when it seems appropriate.

"We're facing a vast subject in a very short time, and this means we'll have to try to stick to the important issues. We're not trying to cover the waterfront, but to open up the subject so you can go on thinking and talking about it."

Pastor Russell pauses briefly and smiles. "It's now my pleasure to introduce Arthur Jones, a specialist in family sociology, and a man known and honored in this community. Dr. Jones."

1

I

Dr. Jones steps up to the stand, puts on his glasses, and spreads out his notes.

"I'm delighted to be invited to share this experience with you. I think the series is an excellent idea, and it looks as though many others do too. My only complaint is that it's tough to try to cover so much material in so short a time, but I'll do my best, and I'll try to avoid being too technical.

"Why did we ever have families at all? The general rule is that the higher the form of life, the longer it takes to grow. Simple creatures are born (or hatched) at a stage of development at which they can take care of themselves. Human babies, by contrast, couldn't possibly survive at birth if left alone. They need to be protected, fed, and kept warm. Who does this? Their parents. When parents take care of their children, we have a family. From a sociological perspective, I believe this is the major function of the family. And that's my first main point.

"A second point. The family is an amazingly old institution. There have been families ever since human beings first appeared—which was at least two million years ago, according to our present knowledge. We can't be sure just what these early families were like, because we have no records. But many experts believe that even the earliest human families were like the families of today—father, mother, and children. They probably lived in caves and managed to survive without any of our modern comforts and conveniences; but the primary *function* of the family was exactly what it is today. Parents cared for their children till they were old enough to care for themselves. So when we think of the awesome fact that the human family has existed for two million years, we realize what a tough and durable institution it is.

"A few years ago, voices were crying out everywhere that traditional family patterns were doomed. I personally think it is highly questionable to say that the family is about to go out of existence. And I'm not alone. I want to quote from an article which appeared in the November 25, 1974 issue of *Time*. The article is entitled 'Avant-Garde Retreat.'

> What is the latest word from the sexual frontier? It may be "retreat."
> Though there is little likelihood that things will go back to where
> they were 30 years ago, the signs are that the sexual avant-

garde—those who practice "swinging," group sex, open marriage, bisexuality and the odder forms of experiment—is in decline. . . .

"There's no doubt that all the experimentation and kinkiness are declining," says Ellen Frankfort, feminist author of *Vaginal Politics*. "Now there's a strong desire for connectedness." Many social scientists, counselors and sex researchers agree. Says Anthropologist Gilbert Bartell, co-author of *Group Sex*: "These are depressed and unsettled times. There's a more somber feeling among people, a retreat from sexual frivolity."

"Having set forth the major function of the family, according to sociology, and affirmed the durability of the family, I now want to make a third point: there are many different kinds of families. We might have expected this of human families because it is true in the animal world. Some animal young are taken care of entirely by their mothers—you know that's how it works out for cats and dogs. But there are families—among fish, for example—where the father takes care of the young. And among the birds, father and mother often work together—building the nest, hatching the eggs, feeding the young.

"Among humans there is yet greater variety. Anthropologists tell us of many types of families: patrilineal families, where the line of descent is traced through the father; matrilineal families, where it is traced through the mother; polygamous families, where one husband lives with several wives or where one wife has several husbands; extended families, with scores of near and distant relatives living together; stem families, where only the eldest son stays at home but where as many as four or five generations may end up under the same roof; and nuclear families, confined to father and mother and those children not yet old enough to leave home. A family can even be two people, husband and wife with no children, a mother and one child, or a father and one child. And if these are families, why not consider apartment-mates unrelated by blood or marriage, but united in friendship, to be a family? Indeed, a person living alone fulfills some characteristics of a family.

"Variety of another sort also exists, for families break up and regroup as parents divorce and remarry; as fathers or mothers desert their children; as new family members are adopted from outside. It's a great mistake to think that all families are of one type, or that all family members remain together throughout their lives. Obviously they don't.

3

"In closing I want to go back to my first point and say a bit more about the family's care of its children. Simple creatures are born with what we call 'instincts.' Who teaches a fly to spread its wings and take to the air? It never sees its parents, so they don't. How does a salmon, swimming in the open sea, know when the time has come to go back to the river where it first hatched out of the egg? And how does it ever find its way there? Today we might say they were 'programmed,' like a computer, to do these things, but instincts are complex and marvelous, and we still don't fully understand how they work.

"We human beings have instincts too—but only a few. Our lives are very complicated and full of choices, so we use our minds instead. But minds need to be trained, and this can only be done by other human beings.

"A king of Scotland once made a rather cruel experiment with a newborn baby whose mother was deaf and dumb. He put them both on a rocky island, with plenty of food. He wanted to see what language the child would speak. You can guess what happened! The child didn't learn to speak at all. We learn to speak only by hearing others speak, and imitating them. That's the way we learn most of the business of living—how to get along with other people, how to tell right from wrong, how to appreciate music, art, and religion, how to feel about ourselves, and what to think about other people.

"In our early years it's at home that we learn most of the basic things we need to know. Then the school takes over and teaches us more of the knowledge the human race has accumulated through the ages. We don't remember most of the learning of our earlier years, but it is of major importance to us because it shapes what we call the unconscious part of our minds. People who don't get that early learning are in bad trouble: they are the people who later suffer from mental and emotional illness.

"In human history we have not found an effective substitute for the family as the means of 'socializing' the child. So sociology says that the family seems to be basic if human culture is to continue. True, there are poorly functioning families that do a poor job, and many of our criminals and social misfits come from such dysfunctional families. But a supportive family provides the necessary setting for the healthy development of human personality."

Dr. Jones turns with a smile. "Doctor, that's my opening statement."

II

Pastor Russell takes his place at the speaker's stand. "Thank you, Dr. Jones. You've given us several fine sociological assertions about the family. I want to add, very briefly, something of what our Christian faith teaches us about the same subject—we'll be dealing with this in more detail in later sessions.

"The Bible begins with the creation story of Adam and Eve in the garden of Eden. God created them, first, to respond to divine love—and I want to affirm that God fully revealed this love in the person of Jesus Christ. As a corollary to this first purpose we Christians believe God created us also to respond to each other.

"Where do we learn how we are to respond? We don't go to the Bible to get all the rules on how to dress, to run schools, to organize hospitals, or to operate airlines. We do find in the Bible principles of conduct God laid down for us. Many of the Bible's specific rules, especially from the Old Testament, are simply ignored in today's world; we do not observe the sacrifices called for in the opening chapters of Leviticus, and many of us right now are violating the last part of Leviticus 19:19, which forbids wearing a garment 'made of two kinds of stuff.' But such Biblical principles as the immediately preceding verse, 'you shall love your neighbor as yourself,' are still the guidelines for our conduct.

"So we do go to the Bible to learn how we, as God's children, are to behave toward each other. Jesus summed up the basis of that conduct in Matthew 22 when, quoting that same Leviticus 19:18, he said that the second great commandment is, 'You shall love your neighbor as yourself.'

"Applied to the family that loves God (the first great commandment), this calls for husbands and wives, parents and children, to live together in love by caring for each other, supporting each other, and forgiving each other.

"I believe this use of Biblical principles is still binding on us, despite the fact that in Bible times the family was very different from the family of today. Young people married in their early teens. Parents usually picked marriage partners for their sons and daughters. Couples were encouraged to have many children— wasn't God's command to the first human couple in Genesis 1: 'Be fruitful and multiply, and fill the earth and subdue it'? Psalm 127 expresses well the Jewish idea of children: 'Lo, sons are a heritage from the LORD, the fruit of the womb a reward. Like arrows in the head of a warrior are the sons of one's youth. Happy is the man who has his quiver full of them!' And why not such an attitude? There was no population problem.

"As children grew up, discipline was firm and punishment could be stern. Remember the text in Proverbs 13 about spanking the children so you wouldn't spoil them? An attitude of obedience and respect was made a condition of the children's prosperity; see the fifth Commandment. Children who dishonored their parents were under divine judgment, and for a child to strike a parent actually could mean his or her execution, according to Exodus 21.

"The honoring of parents by children is reaffirmed in the New Testament, though the harsh penalties are not. In Ephesians 6, the fifth Commandment is cited, with special emphasis on the promise attached to it. But Paul doesn't stop there; he goes on to command parents, 'do not provoke your children to anger, but bring them up in the discipline and instruction of the Lord.' Parents have responsibilities toward their children every bit as much as children have toward their parents.

"This same principle of mutuality should take some of the offense out of Paul's statement, so often quoted in recent days, that wives are to be submissive to their husbands. Three verses later, in Ephesians 5:25, Paul balances that statement with, 'Husbands, love your wives.' This places upon husbands a submissive responsibility to their wives, too!

"These then are some of the principles that the Bible sets forth to help shape the family life of God's people, in order that God's purposes for us may be fulfilled and that our lives may be enriched.

"A second point I want to make tonight about the Christian faith is related to what Arthur Jones has called the major function of the family: caring for the young. From a Christian perspective, we surely accept that concept, but we add to it another dimension.

"In performing the child-raising function, we have an enormous responsibility. We not only contribute to the continuance of human life through our children, but we also transmit our culture, all those truths we hold to be self-evident. But Christians have a double responsibility; we must also pass on our faith in God as he has revealed himself in Jesus Christ. In addition, we seek to develop in our children a sense of 'right' and 'wrong,' an understanding of what it means to love and serve Jesus Christ in today's world."

Pastor Russell pauses as he looks at the people before him. "We also confess that no families do this adequately, but we keep trying! Parenthetically, I think we can find real help in doing this from the Old Testament and from some of our Jewish neighbors. Among devout Jews through the centuries, religious rituals and observances were built into the life of the home. Every father was a kind of priest to his own family. The Jews have kept this up until today. We need to recapture this in the context of our Christian faith.

"I've talked about God's purpose for the family and Biblical principles to guide us, and I've mentioned the need to transmit our Christian faith as well as our Western culture. But there's another side to all of this, if we are going to look at the whole Christian approach to the family. Jesus, so far as we know, never married. He even said that his followers must be prepared to turn their backs on family claims for the sake of the gospel, according to passages found in Luke 9 and Luke 14, and elsewhere.

"Twenty-five years later, Paul, believing that persecution was near (and the end of the world), said it was best for Christians not to take on family responsibilities. He wrote in 1 Corinthians 7, 'I think that in view of the impending distress it is well for a person to remain as he is.' He went on to say that in such times marriage could hinder one from a total commitment to Jesus Christ, and so he suggested that those not already married refrain from it.

"Later in Christian history, this idea of celibacy was interpreted by many in the church as the ideal state for all Christians and all situations. Double standards were set up. A distinction was made between the 'advice' and the 'requirements' of the gospel. Only those who could fulfill lives of voluntary poverty and voluntary celibacy were considered able to fulfill all Christ's commands. By living a life of self-denial, it was taught, these people received special merit. Eventually, in the Western church, priests were forbidden to marry. The most honored Christians were men and women who became monks and nuns, just as we Protestants have given special recognition to missionaries who left homes and comforts for Christ's sake.

"We can partially explain this attitude of de-emphasizing the family. Jesus placed the demands of the gospel before everything else. To make this clear, he selected the dearest human ties and said, in effect, if you are going to be my disciple, even this—your family—must take second place. Thus in a sense he actually showed us how highly he valued the family.

"How do we apply this radical word of the New Testament to ourselves? We certainly don't believe today that there are many situations in which the best way to prove our Christian faith is to walk out on our family obligations! Except in the rarest cases, God's message to us about the family is rooted in the extensive teachings about maintaining and enriching family relationships. The family, indeed, is the place God expects most of us to begin living out our Christian experience. We prove our Christianity by showing love to all the other family members.

"That of course raises another question, as answers often do. What if we don't *feel* loving? Is it wicked to feel anger or hostility toward someone in our home? What can we do about such feelings? Are we to act lovingly even when we don't feel loving? Do we pray for our anger to go away and be replaced with love? Later, we'll be having a whole session about love, but you might want to discuss some of these questions I've raised when you get into your groups.

III

"Now it's time to let you take part in the discussion. Who wants to ask a question?"

"My question is for you, Dr. Russell. We sometimes talk about 'Christian families.' What exactly do we mean by that?"

"I'd say there are two answers to that question. First, there's a pattern of family life that we broadly recognize as Christian. Muslims allow a man to take four wives; Christians permit only one. In some countries where divorce has been almost impossible, a married man sometimes feels it is acceptable to take a mistress, but I don't think we'd say that is appropriate to a Christian pattern of conduct. The writer of Proverbs encourages parents to spank their children, but I don't think it tells husbands to beat their wives, and we would say a family marred by such violence is at best sub-Christian. What I mean is that we have a kind of understanding about what is *not* done in Christian families. This understanding changes, though. Divorce is far more acceptable today than it was when I began my ministry, and this despite such words of Jesus as found in Matthew 19 or Luke 16.

"The second answer to the question may help more. Perhaps

there's no such thing as a Christian family, but rather families in which members are Christians who try to live together in Christian love. It isn't the form that matters—it's the spirit. You could apply this to the African chief who takes three wives and then becomes a Christian. Does he throw out two of his wives and leave them to starve? Or does he cherish all of them in the spirit of Christian love? After all, he could argue that some of the greatest men in the Bible were polygamists, like Abraham and David.!"

"Thank you, pastor."

"Another question?"

"What is the correct number of children for Christian parents to have? I mean, is it un-Christian to have four or five?"

"Dr. Jones, it's your turn."

"Well, we have four children, so it seems I'm on the spot! I notice, however, that the questioner is a young woman—I'd guess she's in her early twenties. Twelve to twenty years ago, when my children were born, few people were talking much about population problems—at least not in the United States. We are now being told that two children per family is the correct size if we are to prevent overcrowding our planet. I certainly think Christians who marry today should give serious consideration to limiting their family's size, although I hope the government will never have to pass a law about it.

"This question is a good example of what your pastor was saying—that we don't govern our lives by literally following instructions the Bible gave to rural communities living in Palestine thousands of years ago. Large families were then the key to survival. People were urged to have large families. Today, the situation is reversed. Small families are the key to survival. It is not a loving act to push future generations in the direction of famine and war."

IV

"I see more hands up, but it's time now to go to our groups. I hope we have given you plenty to talk about. I want to try to pull together some of the issues that have come out of our discussions so far.

"I wonder if you agree with Dr. Jones' statement that the family is basic to the survival of our human culture? How do you deal with the question I raised about Jesus' putting the family in second place? How do we understand his statement in Luke 14 that we must 'hate' our fathers and mothers? Does Paul's belief in imminent persecution and the destruction of the world justify his position on marriage? Do you think that nuns and monks and missionaries are by virtue of their calling more holy than the rest of us Christians? Can one better serve Jesus Christ in an unmarried state?

"What do you feel about using the term 'Christian family'? Do you think our standards have to change—for example, our attitudes toward spanking children? or toward divorce? What would you say to the African chief about his three wives?

"What about feeling angry or hostile toward another family member? Do you ever have such experiences? How do you reconcile anger with Christian love?

"Do you agree that we need small families today? Should Christians limit the number of children they bring into the world? Or do you feel we badly need more real Christians in our world? Would you give a saintly couple a dispensation and allow them to have a large family?

"There are a few questions to start you off. Also, on the board we've listed Biblical passages which were referred to tonight. Now please go to your groups."

Genesis 1:28–2:25
Exodus 20:12; 21:15
Leviticus 19:18–19
Deuteronomy 5:16
Psalm 127: 3–5
Proverbs 13:24
Matthew 5:31–32; 19:3–9; 22:37–40
Luke 9:59–62; 14:26; 16:18
1 Corinthians 7:25–35
Ephesians 5:21–6:9

Chapter 2

Marriage

PASTOR JACK RUSSELL goes to the platform and holds up his hand, waiting for silence.

"Welcome to our second meeting. And a special welcome to those who were not with us last week. We're glad this series on 'Men, Women, and God: Families Today and Tomorrow' is proving popular. You may notice that we've had to bring in extra chairs.

"Our subject for the evening is 'Marriage.' On the panel with me are Dr. Harold Sefton, the new anthropologist on the faculty of Fieldstone College and an Episcopalian, and Mrs. Ruth Wilson, a member of our church who will speak both as a social worker and as a homemaker.

"We'll begin with Dr. Sefton. Welcome, Harold, to our church. We're eager to hear what you have to say."

I

"Thank you, Pastor Russell. This is a good program, and I'm delighted to be taking part in it.

"Anthropologists study human communities of all kinds; and wherever we go, we have always found some form of marriage. However, these forms vary considerably. One culture practices monogamy, another polygamy. In certain places everybody is expected to marry; in others, it's a matter of personal choice. Some peoples make marriage binding for life, others allow divorce and

11

remarriage. In particular cultures partners are chosen for boys and girls, while in many communities they are allowed to choose for themselves. There are cultures where the married couples live with their in-laws; but in our Western practice, normally the newlyweds set up an independent home of their own. There are even places where the woman and man don't live under the same roof at all. Think of almost any variation in the ways a husband and wife could relate to each other, and I suspect we could find a community where it has at least been tried. Marriage is a very flexible institution!

"Why do we have marriage at all? The marriage service in the Episcopalian prayer book cites three reasons: First, to provide for the protection and raising of children; second, to enable people's sexual needs to be met in a way that avoids social complications; third, to encourage the cooperation and companionship of a man and a woman as they set up a home, the social unit on which most human societies have been based.

"Not all Christians agree with the Episcopalian prayer book, especially in its order of priority. When you go into your groups you might like to make that one item for discussion. Possibly you would like to add other reasons why you think marriage is important. I'm giving you only three. I readily admit there are others, though these are pretty basic.

"In the main, Western culture of the past centuries has viewed marriage as the prayer book does. It's put the conception and rearing of children first, and male-female companionship third. Today, it seems to me, our society is reversing that order. I meet more and more couples who are determined to remain childless. This certainly contradicts what many of us have considered to be the basic reason for marriage—to procreate.

"But this is just one among many changes. So many of our traditional concepts of marriage are being seriously challenged. For example, it's been argued that parents are not necessarily the best people to raise their children, and that it could be handled better by the state or community. Another position taken is that the new sexual freedom, because of the availability of contraceptives and abortion, makes it unnecessary for people to marry for sex, and if they want variety in relationships they can get it better outside marriage. Marriage is also rejected for other reasons. It's blamed because some married couples fail to find satisfying companionship and just make each other miserable. Some advocates of liberation have claimed that marriage has been used by men to keep women in subjection.

"For these and other reasons, some people today favor doing away with marriage as we have known it in the past, and replacing it with freer patterns of relationship between men and women. Others argue instead that marriage still meets the deepest needs of most people for intimacy and companionship, but that we must do more to help married couples achieve this goal.

"For the anthropologist, the idea of replacing marriage as we have known it with other arrangements raises some very searching questions. As I pointed out, we have always found marriage in some form in all the human cultures we have studied. The forms have been very different but marriage and the family have been and are the primary channels through which the culture is transmitted from generation to generation. The child learns at home, through thousands of daily impressions, an awareness of self, of maleness and femaleness, of what it means to be white or black or red, to be an American, to be married, to be a parent, et cetera. These learnings all contribute to the kind of adult the child becomes.

"If we change the cultural pattern, all this will be broken down and something else will emerge in its place. That something else may be *better* than what we have now, but it may turn out to be *worse*. We could produce new types of personality with new and different motives, values, and behavior patterns. We just don't know how this would work out. We have never before experienced cultural change taking place on such a broad scale and at such a rapid rate. We might end up with the kind of idealistic society the starry-eyed young people in the communes talk about. At the other extreme, we might tear down the foundations of Western culture as it has developed over thousands of years and have nothing of equal worth to put in its place.

"All I'm saying is that we ought to face these facts. Marriage is a very basic institution. It's one of the nuclear human relationships. Any major change will have very profound effects on all other human relationships.

"At the same time, I recognize that very significant changes are taking place in our marriage patterns. This is almost inevitable. What concerns me is that the changes be in the right direction—

toward the *improvement* of the man-woman relationship and of society. I wouldn't want to make changes so quickly or violently that we can't assimilate them."

II

"Thank you, Dr. Sefton. Now I'll attempt to relate the Christian faith to marriage; I intend to speak briefly, since when I spoke last week on the family I dealt with marriage too.

"As Dr. Sefton said, things are changing and some think changing too quickly. A few of our friends here at First Church already talk as if they think the world is coming to an end. Even meetings like this are comparatively new; if our Christian forebears could come back and hear public talk about marriage and sex—and in the church—they would likely be horrified.

"In the past our Christian standard of marriage has been a very strict one, and it has been rigidly enforced. While examples could be cited to the contrary, I think that these three standards have been generally applied: We have demanded absolute monogamy—the union of one man and one woman for life; we have upheld chastity and fidelity—no sex relations of any kind either before marriage or outside marriage; and third, we must acknowledge that the concept of Christian marriage has largely expected the husband to be dominant and the wife submissive.

"But there's another side of the story that we don't often hear these days. The Christian marriage standard was strict because the Christian marriage ideal was high. The early church spoke out against the background of a pagan world which put a low value on married love, on womanhood, and on child life. The church wasn't making rules for the world in general; it was setting up standards for Christian believers. Paul in Ephesians called on husbands to love their wives with the same devotion as Christ's love for the church. In marriages where husband and wife were dedicated to making each other happy, the Christian standard created no problems. A loving husband wouldn't exploit his trusting wife. A loving wife would support her husband and would not seek to manipulate him.

"Tertullian wrote in the second century:

How beautiful is the marriage of two Christians, two who are one in hope, one in desire, one in the way of life they follow, one in the religion they practice . . . . Nothing divides them, either in flesh or in spirit. They pray together; instructing one another, encouraging one another, strengthening one another . . . . They have no secrets from one another; they never shun each other's company; they never bring sorrow to each other's hearts. They visit the sick and assist the needy. Psalms and hymns they sing to one another, striving to see which of them will chant more beautifully the praises of their Lord. Hearing and seeing this, Christ rejoices. To such as these He gives His peace. Where there are two together there also He is present.

"This is a Christian marriage ideal. Some will find it beautiful and heartwarming, while others will dismiss it as sentimental and unreal. But before we condemn the church too harshly, we do need to keep the church's good intention in mind, as it faced a pagan world and sought to build strong homes.

"We'll talk in later sessions about both sex and woman-man relationships. Tonight I'll say a little more about absolute monogamy and the permanence of marriage—the first of the three standards I listed as I began.

"It must be admitted that too often the church has been content to put its emphasis on stringent rules about divorce instead of moving in with help and support as people realized their inability to live up to the high ideal of marriage.

"Karl Barth, the Swiss Reformed theologian, complained that the traditional church was not concerned with marriages, only with weddings. By that he meant that ecclesiastical authorities held rigidly to the legal requirements, but turned a blind eye to the *relationship* between husband and wife. No matter how miserable the couple were together, as long as they kept up the outward appearance of a secure and stable marriage, that was all that mattered.

"Today this whole approach has been challenged, if not blown sky-high, in a world where many are insisting that good relationships are more important than stable institutions.

"This confronts us Christians with a painful choice. *Isn't* the stability of the institution more important than the quality of the relationship? Didn't Jesus say plainly that for Christians there must be no divorce?

"Here's an idea for you to think about. We know that Jesus was a Jew who observed the Law of Moses. On one occasion. his disciples ate grain from the fields on the sabbath day. That was strictly forbidden. The religious leaders challenged him. 'Look, why are they doing what is not lawful on the sabbath?'

"I'd like to read Jesus' answer. The whole incident is found in Mark with parallels in Matthew and Luke.

> And he said to them, "Have you never read what David did, when he was in need and was hungry, he and those who were with him: how he entered the house of God, when Abiathar was high priest, and ate the bread of the Presence, which it is not lawful for any but the priests to eat, and also gave it to those who were with him?" And he said to them, "The sabbath was made for man, not man for the sabbath; so the Son of man is lord even of the sabbath."

"What did Jesus mean? He put the needs of human beings above the rigors of the Law. He was more concerned about human values than about the legal system. Would it be Christian for us to apply the same principle to marriage? Would it be in the spirit of Jesus' teaching to say that marriage was made for people and not people for marriage?

"That's what many voices are saying today with our more open attitudes to marriage. But we have an uncomfortable feeling sometimes that we're letting down our Christian forebears. And when we find that the more freedom we allow, the more people demand, we have misgivings about how far we ought to go in relaxing the rigid rules of the past.

"But now I'm touching on the practical level, so I'll turn the discussion over to Mrs. Wilson."

III

Petite Ruth Wilson adjusts the microphone to her height.

"I speak as a happily married woman. But in my job as a family caseworker, I see plenty of people who are disenchanted with marriage. Or rather, I should say they are disenchanted with the particular marriage they're in. It's important to make that distinction. I find that people whose marriages break up still long for a good relationship with others. Statistics show that most divorced people remarry within a few years. Part of that could be explained by the pressure of society—our culture *is* largely geared toward couples and families. But even allowing for that, it seems that the ideal of marriage represents a very deep human need, and that we pursue it with a hope that isn't easily abandoned.

"I myself, and most of the couples I know, would like to have really good marriages. This isn't easy to achieve. It may be that we are asking too much of marriage. We have made it all sound very romantic, as if being in love was a guarantee of lifelong happiness. I can tell you that this isn't true. Most of the couples I deal with were very much in love, or thought they were, when they started. After a few years their dreams were shattered. So I've had to ask myself: 'Are we expecting too much? Have we oversold marriage?'

"To some extent I'm sure we have. Yet from my own experience I know that marriage can come up to all our expectations. It can be beautiful and it can be wonderful. Marriage can fulfill that description our pastor read to us. So why isn't it like that for *all* of us?

"There may be many answers. First, I don't really believe marriage is for everyone. Some can't adjust to a close relationship with another person. They're 'loners' by nature. Second, there are married people who simply don't suit each other: their temperaments clash; they constantly disagree. Sometimes people like that divorce and do better in a second marriage. But, third, the problem for most people is that they don't know how to make a marriage work. They can't communicate. They can't cooperate. They can't express their true feelings. They become frustrated and blame each other. If they get to a marriage counselor in time, they can sometimes save the situation. Often they seek help too late.

"Society may be to blame for many marriage failures. We don't help young people understand the complexity of interpersonal relationships. We don't adequately prepare them for marriage. We consider marriage to be such a private and personal matter that we shut the couple up in a box and leave them to work it out for themselves. We often create the impression that marriage requires no special knowledge or skill, that it 'comes natural'; therefore, we imply, anyone who needs help must be weak and incompetent. As a result, by the time they're absolutely desperate and have to seek help, it's too late.

"More couples could be successful in marriage if we recognized that it's a difficult but very worthwhile task—something we need to learn about in order to manage successfully."

"Thank you, Ruth."

IV

"Now that you've heard our three statements, I think it's time to let you ask questions. Who's first?"

"I'd like to ask Mrs. Wilson if she thinks marriage exploits women."

"Yes, I think it sometimes does. I don't feel exploited. My husband and I have always regarded our marriage as a partnership of equals. I gave up working when our children were small, because I wanted to stay home and enjoy them. I felt they needed me. When they were all at school I went back to my career, and my husband expressed full approval.

"However, other wives are less fortunate; their husbands aren't so understanding. Traditional concepts of marriage are based on the idea that the husband is a superior person. Our laws and customs have certainly supported that idea. However, I don't think that means we ought to give up on marriage as an outdated institution. We need to make changes. We need to educate people. Laws need revision. Customs need serious rethinking. Certainly many women feel exploited in marriage.

"However, had you asked me if marriage exploits men, I'd answer the same way. Any marriage that belittles, dehumanizes or de-emphasizes an individual's sense of worth is exploitive.

"I suppose the best way to answer is simply to say, any human relationship is subject to exploitation. I am committed—as many are today—to finding ways to help people actualize the kind of partnership they want. Some of us have already found it. We hope our experiences can help others."

"Thank you, Ruth. Another question?"

"Pastor, my question is this: In the past—especially in our country—when strict standards were imposed on everyone, did this really work?"

Pastor Russell smiles. "I think you probably know the answer to that one. Human nature is still human nature and that hasn't changed much over the epochs of time."

The questioner smiles in return, nodding her head.

"Of course, the strict rules didn't work—at least not for everyone. Behind the scenes, all the rules were broken. Young people experienced premarital sex. Husbands went to prostitutes or even kept mistresses. Wives took lovers. Unhappy couples drifted apart and lived, secretly or openly, with other partners. It was all a matter of how strongly the culture imposed its penalties, and how much fear people had of breaking out of prescribed norms.

"One further comment, however. Even if marriages are only

held together by fear, at least that keeps families stable, and results in a more orderly and disciplined society. The question we are having to ask today is, how much freedom can we allow and still hold society together? Frankly, we just don't know the answer."

"Pastor, are you saying that you advocate stability *at any cost?*"

"No, that's not quite what I'm saying. I only point out that the more strict the rules, it seems to me, the more stable the families. How important is stability in any society? Is stability so important that we must sacrifice personhood? Or if affirmation of persons rates top priority, are we willing to pay that price? Or do you think I'm overstating the situation? This is another area your groups might wish to discuss."

V

"And now we've run out of time. We'll break up and go into our groups. I want to throw out a few additional questions and I hope you'll pursue them.

"All three of us have pointed out that marriage faces a crisis in the world today. How do we, individually, as members of society, and as Christians, meet this crisis? How far can we still insist on the standards which we have accepted in American culture—lifelong monogamy, premarital chastity, marital fidelity? Is this still the standard for others? How does this affect our attitudes to others?

"If your unmarried daughter lives with a young man, do you disown her? Tell her you disapprove and settle for that? Turn a blind eye? If a church official gets divorced, should he resign? If a wife who is a church member leaves her husband, and a year later brings a new husband with her to church, should we make them welcome?

"Suppose two people living together should ask to become church members? They feel married in the sight of God, and refuse to go through the legal ceremony; should we turn them away? What if a family of church members doesn't conform to what we consider normal standards of loving relationships? What attitude do we take?

"We've also talked about helping marriages become better. We've mentioned educating young people before they reach the stage of marriage. We've also talked of counseling for marriages. How else might we help marriages become stronger? If it's all a matter of giving people proper help to make their marriages successful and fulfilling, what does that involve? What should we as a church be doing that we aren't doing?

"Again on the board we've listed the Biblical passages referred to tonight or that might be helpful in your discussion."

Genesis 2:18–25
Matthew 5:31–32; 19:3–9
Mark 2:23–28
Romans 12:9–21
1 Corinthians 12:14–13:13
Ephesians 5:21–33

Chapter 3

Parenthood

PASTOR JACK RUSSELL glances at his watch, breaks off a conversation, and comes to the front.

"Your planning committee talked for some time about how to get us started on this complex subject of parenthood. We finally decided we would like a couple to lead the session, and that three areas should be covered. First, we'd like a report on what child development sciences see happening. Second, we want to look at the distinctive concerns the Christian faith raises when the subject of parenthood comes up. Third, we want a reaction from a parent who has some knowledge of both these areas.

"Jane and Jim Darnell are our leaders, and the last two areas will be presented by Jane. Now Jim Darnell will start us off by talking about what he's learned from the specialists in the field of child development."

I

Jim with a grin lays a number of 3 × 5 cards on the stand.

"I took the easy way out and talked to one specialist, Dr. Evelyn Whittier at the junior college. What stood out for me from our conversation was her emphasis on the dramatic effect of a changing world on the raising of children. True, we're all aware of changes, and most of us who are parents find ourselves pretty uneasy about a lot of them. But Dr. Whittier made me more keenly aware of this than I ever had been before.

"What are some of these changes? To begin with, we've gone from the large-sized family to the small, from closed families to open families, from strict discipline to permissiveness. And divorce is more and more common.

"Let's look closer at some of these. From the pioneer days on in America, families were large. Children were greatly desired—they helped on the farm and increased its productivity. They didn't have to be sent to college and so they didn't drain the family budget. In a sense, the children provided the only Social Security people could count on in their old age.

"All that has now changed. The command of Genesis 1:28, 'Be fruitful and multiply,' used to be the prescription for survival and mutual helpfulness. Now the prescription is zero population growth. That means two children per couple, and so parenthood in our time must be planned.

"There's general agreement among child development specialists that the ideal setting for healthy child development is two loving parents, mutually fulfilled in their marriage, who can provide their children with an overflow of warm, non-possessive love. In such families the children identify positively with parents of their own sex, and learn by observation how to relate positively to parents of the opposite sex.

"Children who grow up in happy, complete, nuclear families unconsciously learn the roles they will later need in marriage and parenthood. They also gain a deep, satisfying sense of worth and a respect for others who share their lives. Such experiences help make them mature, self-confident adults, capable of relating positively and creatively to other people, not only in the small world of the home but in the larger outside community.

"Nowadays, though, fewer and fewer children are having the opportunities of growing up in this ideal setting. Our high rate of marital breakdowns means that large numbers of children spend at least some years of their lives in one-parent families, and that parent often is going through considerable emotional stress. Others have to part company with one parent following divorce and adjust to a step-parent, as well as to other children brought into the new family circle created by remarriage. These experiences often mean traumatic changes and a loss of security. While children suffer in homes if their parents are in conflict, they also suffer if their parents' marriage breaks up.

"Even when family members stay together, the task of modern parents is much more complicated than it used to be.

"Consider the outside influences working on our children, like TV, the youth culture, or our financial affluence. Margaret Mead said that many parents just stand on the sidelines in a state of exasperated helplessness while their children are raised by the mass media!

"In small families the children often seek close companions outside the home. This seems especially true when a family's children are widely separated in age or are of different sex. This means that the values taught in the home are likely to be contradicted by different values which their companions have picked up in their families. At quite an early age children sense this conflict of loyalties. The conflict grows acute for adolescents, who in gaining independence may find themselves more and more alienated from parents. When this conflict reaches crisis proportions, we often see it unhappily resolved by teenagers running away. This has become so common that many parents dread the time when their children will reach adolescence."

A hand shoots up from the rear.

"Pardon me for interrupting. I realize we'll have time for questions later, but I'm really bothered. You make it sound so—so pessimistic—as though it hardly does any good to teach our children because by the time they reach their teen years, outside influences will have counteracted everything we've done."

"I'm sorry if I've given that impression. That's not the one Dr. Whittier gave me. Actually, I'm trying to present a balanced picture. It's not easy to raise children. There are a lot of counteracting influences. But I am also strongly committed to the fact that we don't have to give up.

"Now if you're looking for a set of rules or a new method on how to be good parents, I don't have anything for you. Frankly, no one knows precisely what makes the difference between being a good parent and an almost-good parent. Certainly, caring for the children physically and emotionally, and encouraging them toward confidence, strength, and faith are all part of it. All parents make mistakes, of course, but we believe that God can do something even with these. There are no easy rules or formulas for successful parenting. Having and showing a capacity for loving and enjoying the growth of those in your care—that's about the best advice I can offer.

"Another problem caused by these changes is the breakdown of parental discipline. Children need control. Their unbridled impulses can lead into trouble. They can best learn self-discipline with the cooperation of wise parents. Parents in the past generally exercised discipline in an authoritarian manner. Most modern parents reject autocratic rule, but have never been taught the more difficult cooperative method. As a result, many give up in despair and become what we term permissive, which really means indulgent, allowing children to do whatever they wish. These young people, then, learn no inner control, which only intensifies their alienation from their parents and their parents' way of life."

"Excuse me for interrupting you again. When you say something I'm not clear about or I disagree with, I want to ask you now. You've mentioned the cooperative method of discipline. You say it as though everyone knew what you meant. I sure don't!"

"Thank you—I'm glad you called me on that.

"By the cooperative method I mean communication and interaction with the children. This means no longer demanding unquestioning obedience, because we no longer see the job of parenthood as just an effort to subdue the children's will.

"Many parents today are plagued with doubts about whether they are doing the right thing. In our family we've tried to talk things over with our children, especially when there is disagreement. When I feel I have to override them, I try to explain carefully so they understand my decision.

"Another thing we do is ask their opinion about punishments for disobedience. I've discovered that my children have a sharp sense of justice. If they feel they deserve punishment, they'll say so. My little Julie, at age five, speaks up. If she thinks we're being unfair, she is allowed to express that. My wife and I try to give our children the opportunity to convince us. We want to be open-minded about it.

"Perhaps that gives you an idea of what we mean by cooperative discipline. We work with the children. It's certainly better than the authoritarian kind where mother or father makes a decision and the children are just to give unquestioning obedience."

"But children *are* immature. They don't understand all the implications of their decisions."

"Exactly. That's why we call it cooperative and not democratic. My wife and I have not abdicated our position of responsibility. We call in the children to get their viewpoints. We try to listen. But we still make the final decisions. For our family, it works. And, I want to add, it's made things a lot easier around the house. The kids recognize our attempt at fairness. I can't recall their ever objecting or calling us unfair when we've talked things over with them. But in the few instances when I've rushed in and started handing our punishment, they've called me on it! It's precisely because of their acute sense of justice that we can work this method successfully.

"These problems are all part of what we call the 'generation gap.' Our very rapid rate of social change has produced a situation in which parents and children live in two different worlds—the parents in the rejected past, their children in the uncharted future. Margaret Mead has said that today's roles are reversed. Instead of parents bringing up their children, modern children must try to bring up their parents.

"There was a lot more in my conversation with Dr. Whittier, but I'll stop with a word I personally found comforting in a scary way: Dr. Whittier believes that while parenthood has never been easy, never in the world's history has the task been more difficult than at the present."

II

"Thanks, Jim. Now we'll give Jane Darnell the opportunity to speak. She is the mother of three children, besides being the Minister of Education in our church. Jane, what help can you give us on parenthood from the standpoint of the Christian faith?"

"To begin with, the Bible speaks clearly that both parents are to love their children. We're all familiar with passages about God's *fathering* love. I want merely to point out that despite the fact that the Hebrews lived in a patriarchal society and regarded women as weaker beings, there are some passages in the Bible where God is compared to a mother.

"One passage is Hosea 11:3–4: 'Yet it was I who taught Ephraim to walk, I took them up in my arms; but they did not know that I healed them. I led them with cords of compassion, with the bands of love.' This shows God doing what we normally consider the feminine tasks of teaching the child to walk and nurturing.

"Even clearer is Isaiah 49:15: 'Can a woman forget her sucking child, that she should have no compassion on the son of her womb? Even these may forget, yet I will not forget you.' That verse seems self-evident. What I'm trying to point out is that we need to think of God as Parent and not just as Father, and this helps stress the significance of parenthood in the history of the people of God.

"I deliberately said people of God instead of just Christians, because we must acknowledge our debt to the Hebrews, who held a profound sense of the religious significance of being a parent.

"The Old Testament begins with the account of creation. The Hebrews never lost their sense of wonder that God made humanity in his own image. For them, having and rearing children was the continuing by human beings of the work of God. Hebrews considered procreation as God's delegation of his work as creator to people. So, for the Hebrew, parenthood was the most godlike function of which women and men were capable.

"The Hebrews loved children and earnestly desired them. For them, fulfillment after death was to live on through their children and their children's children. In turn, the children's duty was to continue the family line and to preserve their heritage. If children departed from the values of their parents, this brought sorrow and disgrace upon the family.

"Christians shared these concerns, and this led many of them to adopt a strict disciplinary code in raising their children. Above all, Christian parents were expected to bring up their children 'in the discipline and instruction of the Lord' as Paul says it in Ephesians 6. It was considered a mark of serious failure if their children grew up to be unbelievers.

"Our liberal concepts today challenge this strict tradition. Respect for the unique individuality of children and their right to go their own ways and 'do their own thing' hits head-on the more traditional idea in Proverbs 22 that parents must 'train up a child in the way he should go'; that if they spare the rod, they'll spoil the child, according to Proverbs 13. Parents who follow the stringent patterns have no sympathy with the idea of cooperating with children, because they feel that undermines their sense of their own authority and power. On the other hand, parental authority works only when children either are willing to accept it, or are compelled to because they have no allies to support their resistance. Our modern culture provides children and youth with very strong allies, so that as they grow older, parental authority tends to lose its power and influence."

"Excuse me, please," a voice says from the right side of the room. "I'm no expert, but I'd like to say something about this matter of parenthood."

"Of course, Mr. Thompkins."

"I'm not trying to brag. At least I hope I'm not. But my wife and I have always been concerned about raising our children to love

26

God. We've tried in all kinds of ways—in everything that happened in our home—to bring God in. I don't mean just when we had family devotions, although we had them, too.

"We tried to bring God into our decisions and our conversations. Not by threatening the children, but I mean by making Jesus Christ a partner to the discussion. So when they made their beds or talked 'kid talk,' we'd try to bring Jesus Christ into the conversation. We wanted our children to gain a close feeling to God and to know he was there to depend on. We didn't raise any perfect kids, but I'm proud of the ones we have!"

"I gather, Mr. Thompkins, that part of what you're saying is that you had times of formal instruction. But you also believe that your children learned a lot about what to value even when they weren't explicitly being taught."

"Yes, that's a good way of saying it. Mary and I tried to make our commitment clear to our children. We learned from them, too, as we went along. We tried to *live* the kinds of lives we wanted our children to imitate."

III

"Thanks, Mr. Thompkins. And perhaps this is a good place to change directions in my presentation on parenthood and move from a focus on Christian concerns to day-by-day issues as seen in the light of child development and of distinctively Christian insight. The solutions to the problems of parenthood have to be found in practice and not just in theory.

"Some parents seem to make parenthood difficult for themselves. In our home, our children seem to have made it easier. We thank God for that and for them.

"I've talked this all over with Jim and with the children. The ideas I now want to share with you came partly from them and in consultation with them.

"Jim and I have always accepted the Hebrew idea of our children as a gift from God. We welcomed them and expected to enjoy them. Our expectation has not been in vain—our children have given us a great deal of real, deep happiness. With a sense of wonder we have watched them grow and mature. And we have always let them know that we enjoyed them. That may seem a small thing, but I think it's very important.

"Children are also a sacred trust, and we have taken our obli-

27

gations as parents seriously. We have tried, as the hymn says, to 'lose the duty in the joy.'

"Another thing we have stressed is our own cooperation as parents. This isn't easy for us. Jim's work is demanding, and my busiest times are weekends, just when most people are together as a family. But Jim and I have always tried to make time to be with our children. Sometimes Jim does things with them when I'm not along. As Evelyn Whittier pointed out to Jim, it's important for children to have *two* parents, and two parents who really share the experience.

"We've always tried to be united in our decisions about the children, and to support each other whenever either of us had to punish a child. We feel that this gives our children a secure feeling. They know that the rules are dependable.

"As to cooperating with the children, we've done our best. We've tried to talk things over with them whenever we had any disagreement. Another thing we've done has been to ask their opinion about punishments, as Jim explained. This was his idea, and I had great doubts about whether it would work. I was mistaken, and I can now say it has worked for us.

"Anyone would think to hear me talk, that we knew all the answers and had no problems. That's far from being true. One area where we feel we have failed is in family devotions. It seems right and natural for members of a Christian family to worship together, and we've tried a lot of methods. But they haven't been very successful. The wide age differences make it difficult to keep everyone interested. When some members of the family grow obviously bored, that tends to spoil it for the others. If anyone has a sure-fire solution for *that* problem, we'd be very glad to hear about it.

"We have other problems, too. In our world today there are so many things being said and done against our values that we sometimes wish we could not only communicate values better but protect our children from adverse influences. Life today is pretty mind-stretching. With a great effort we try to be a shade more tolerant about something—like marihuana or homosexuality—and no sooner do we reduce our so-called 'rigidity' by one notch than the pressure is on to let it out another notch. It's hard not to lose patience and go back to a hard line.

"So it's hard to be good Christian parents these days. But we don't intend to give up. We find it a challenge. And when the kids really run us ragged, we always get back into balance by asking each other the question—'So what? Would it have been better not to have had children at all?' There's never any doubt about the answer to *that* question."

Jane Darnell sits down and Pastor Russell returns to the speaker's desk.

IV

"We haven't solved all the problems of parenthood in three short speeches, but you know better than to expect that anyway. Now, do you have any questions or comments?"

"Yes, I'd like to react to the idea of parents' presenting a united front on issues. It seems to me that if parents always agree with one another, they don't present their real selves to their children. And in fact they *don't* always agree, so wouldn't it be more honest to admit it? It could be helpful for a boy to know that his father takes his side when his mother doesn't. That makes them more real as people. Also, it doesn't draw a sharp line between the adult world and the child world, but enables the lines of division to be split in other directions. I think it's a point worth considering, although it might be disturbing if it happened too often. I believe it gives children a sense of security when their parents are *generally* in agreement, but it may become artificial if they *always* agree. No two honest individuals could possibly always agree!"

Pastor Russell notes, "That was helpful. Anyone else?"

"I'd like to put on the agenda for some more discussion the matter about communication between parents and youth. I don't doubt that there's a generation gap, but I still think there's far *more* communication between the generations now than we've ever had before. When I was a child—and I'm nearly 60 now—parents and children communicated very little. My parents presented an air of complete infallibility; they gave orders which we were expected to obey right away. There was no discussion, no answering back. 'Children should be seen and not heard' was the rule in our house.

"What we have now is the opening up of the channels of communication between parents and children. But a great deal of the communication taking place is *negative*. Parents often say their children don't communicate. The truth is that the parents often don't want to listen to what the children have to say. This discourages children from even trying! The children, believing that what the parents say to them is always negative, don't want to listen either."

"So what should be done about it?" calls out another voice.

"The only way out I know is for both parents and children to agree that they'll take turns in listening to each other, and won't argue until they have heard it all. If all the negative things on both sides can be said and listened to, the channels are then cleared for more positive communication. It's very hard to do, I admit. But it can work."

"May I make a general comment as a grandmother? I know raising children is difficult these days, but I want to remind younger couples that putting your best into parenthood is like investing money. Years later, you get it back with interest. When your children are grown up, and have children of their own, their love and gratitude is one of life's most precious rewards. I know, because I'm enjoying that experience now. That was all I wanted to say."

"I wanted to add something, too. Joe and I started to skip this session because we not only have no children but plan never to have any for what we consider good reasons. Incidentally, in spite of all the talk about children holding the family together, recent studies we've seen show that childless marriages are on the whole a shade happier than marriages with children. Sometimes the strain and tension of children *weaken* the relationship between husband and wife. Whether that's reason enough to have no children is another question—it wasn't what motivated us. But we're glad we came"—Joe nods his agreement—"both because we are considering adoption and because we've gotten a better understanding of our friends, children and adults. And we'd be interested in some reaction to our decision to have no children of our own."

Jim stands up once again.

"Before we get our list of other issues to talk about, I want to mention one more thing that Dr. Whittier said. When we started talking, she joked about child specialists having badly behaved children, sort of the way some preachers talk about preachers' kids. But later she came back to that subject to say that that shouldn't be true. As a mother she had found it enormously helpful to understand her own children's development, to know what was going on in their lives. This often enabled her to be more patient and to act more sensibly than she would otherwise have done. She hopes her students, as a result of what they learn together, will also be better parents. It can hardly be otherwise. It's logical that you do any job better when you understand in depth what is going on. Universal parent education would be a vast and important step forward. She thinks its bound to come eventually."

"Fine, Jim.

V

"Now let's add a few more items to the list of things we hope to discuss. We've already got more than we can handle. What is unique or even special about *Christian* parenthood? I guess everyone accepts family planning, but what about abortion? How can unmarried mothers, parents without partners, or step-parents handle their especially complicated responsibilities? Can the churches give them any special help?

"Are there new ways of discipline that work better today than the old ways? How can parents best communicate their faith to their children? How do they deal with the rejection of religion by their children, which so often happens?

"And we have a few Biblical references that you may want to study or at least reread as you talk about parenthood."

Genesis 1:28
Proverbs 13:24; 22:6
Isaiah 49:15
Hosea 11:3–4
Ephesians 6:4
Some Biblical parents: Rebekah & Isaac (Jacob) Genesis 25:21; 27:1–28:5
Jacob & (stepmother) Leah (Joseph) Genesis 37
Hannah & Elkanah (Samuel) 1 Samuel 1:1–2:21
David & Maacah (Absalom) 2 Samuel 3:3; 13:1–18:33

Chapter 4

Sex

"OUR GUEST SPECIALIST tonight is Dr. Willard Franklin, head psychiatrist of the Gordon Clinic. Dr. Franklin has had extensive experience in dealing with human sex problems. He recently helped train faculty counselors at Fieldstone College to deal with student sex problems, so he comes well informed.

"After discussion about our meeting, Dr. Franklin and I agreed that it might be best for me to give the opening talk this time.

I

"Throughout most of Christian history," Pastor Russell continues, "sex has been a rather painful subject to discuss openly. I want to do the best I can to explain why.

"Last week, when Jane Darnell was talking about Christian parenthood, she explained how the ancient Hebrews thought of procreation as the way in which men and women took over God's original work of creation. So for the Hebrews there couldn't be anything unspiritual about sex. When a husband and wife were having intercourse, they were doing God's work. Related to this is the fact that circumcision was the Old Testament rite by which a boy was accepted into the Jewish congregation. It meant the offering to God of a part of the organ with which the boy would later do God's work and become a father.

"So we find the Old Testament speaking about sex in a very

natural, open way. Of course sex could be misused, and this was as sinful as the misuse of any of God's other gifts. But sex itself was intended for good. The Hebrews didn't feel either embarrassed or negative about it. The New Testament has a similar approach; thus 1 Timothy 4 describes marriage as God's gift to be received with thanksgiving, and Hebrews 13 speaks of marriage, including the marriage bed, as honorable.

"As the Christian church spread out into the Roman Empire, however, this tended to change. There isn't time to go into details, but we now know that frequently the church's teaching about sex, as about other subjects, was affected by the life-styles and philosophies of its pagan surroundings.

"In the Roman Empire many undesirable sex practices were going on, and converts to the Christian faith had to be persuaded to give up the bad habits of their earlier pagan lives.

"So Paul deals specifically with sexual issues in 1 Corinthians. In chapter 5, he refers to the case of a professing Christian who is living with his father's wife—probably a stepmother. In chapter 6, he speaks out against quite a number of sexual practices that some of the Corinthian believers formerly practiced. In chapter 7, he recognizes the constant temptation to immorality they faced.

"Such passages make clear the difference between the standards required of the professing Christians in Corinth and those of the pagan community in which they lived.

"Of more serious long-range harm was the effect of certain schools of Greek philosophy that tended to despise the body and the things of the body. Some had taken a radical position which said, 'The body is utterly unimportant; therefore we can do what we like with it. Sex is as natural as eating and is to be enjoyed as freely. Only the body is affected, so no moral issue (or sin) can be involved.'

"That same Greek idea led some to the other extreme: 'The body is evil. Therefore we must bring it into total subjection. We must completely deny all the instincts and desires which are natural to the body.' Read aright, the New Testament rejects both the promiscuity of the former position and the total asceticism of the latter.

"However, in its early centuries the church began to go beyond just condemning the evil sex practices of the pagan world, and eventually it began to teach the un-Biblical, ascetic idea that sex itself was evil. This idea took hold, and soon priests were forbidden to marry. Extremists even went so far as to regard sex as the original sin, and to assert that only unmarried monks and nuns could be really spiritual. You can see how far Christians in the Western world had departed from the original Hebrew idea that husband and wife in their sex life were doing God's work and receiving his special blessing.

"Even when Martin Luther defied the Roman church and allowed Protestant pastors to marry, the old, ugly attitude kept creeping back. Many sects arose which saw the world, the human body, and especially sex as contaminated by sin and evil—completely denying God's own pronouncement at the creation when he called it good.

"Today we live in the time of the 'sexual revolution,' when such negative and repressive attitudes have been seriously challenged in the name of scientific knowledge and human values. As nearly always happens, extremists have gone too far in the other direction, and sex, for long centuries suppressed, has now been publicly paraded in the most vulgar manner. We need somehow to put sex in its proper place as a normal, natural part of human nature. There are encouraging signs indicating that we are beginning to move in this direction.

"Because of all that has happened, one of the tasks facing Christians today is to re-examine our traditional teaching about sex—to sift out what is not Christian teaching at all, and to decide what is. This will not be an easy task. Many of us are still emotionally affected by the attitude that anything sexual is sinful, that even to discuss sex is shameful, and that we are in some way guilty if we show any interest in the subject.

II

"We now turn to our task this evening, which is to try to discover an enlightened, informed Christian attitude to sex. The next step in that direction is to hear, from an authority on the subject, a brief summary of the scientific facts about human sexuality. Dr. Franklin, we're grateful to have you with us."

"Thank you, Pastor Russell.

"Human sexuality is a vast subject; in a short talk I can only touch on a few aspects of it. I will leave out entirely the subject of reproduction—the 'facts of life,' as it used to be called—assuming that what you are concerned about is sexual behavior.

"Sexual intercourse is a subject we have not been very comfortable about discussing, and yet, if you will give it a moment's thought, you will realize that in one sense it is the most important subject of all. If a magician cast a spell on the earth and caused all sexual intercourse to cease, that would be the end of human history.

"It is nature's first responsibility, therefore, to take good care of sex and to see that it works properly. This is done by insuring that long before babies are born they are well equipped with reproductive organs; by endowing us with very powerful sexual drives; and by making it possible for us to function sexually throughout a large part of the life-span.

"It was once thought that children had no interest in sex until they reached puberty, but sixty years ago Freud startled the world by proving that infants have sexual feelings. Many of us still think of grade-school children as indifferent to sex, although that really isn't true. Our cultural morality assumed that teenagers could 'tune out' all sexual feelings till they got married in their twenties—but it's now known that boys reach the peak of their sexual power at about the age of 18. In the Victorian era it was considered unladylike for married women to experience any pleasant feelings during intercourse. We now know that some women are capable of higher levels of sexual response than men.

"All along the line, the power of the sex drive was grossly underestimated, and what were considered correct patterns of sexual behavior then were based on that inaccurate picture. Suppose we planned our eating arrangements on the assumption that human beings needed only one meal a day, or suppose we persuaded ourselves that it was bad for our physical health to sleep more than four hours a night. You know what would happen, don't you? People would be eating snacks privately behind locked doors, or secretly napping in the bathtub. And we'd develop all kinds of guilty feelings about food or sleep.

"Another aspect of traditional sex morality was the belief that no sex act could be right unless it took place under conditions in which conception could occur. This was logical at a time when death-rates were high and the only way to keep up the population was to see that as many babies as possible were born. A policy like that would be absolutely suicidal today on our already overcrowded planet—unless every fertile young married couple were willing to have sexual intercourse only during a total period of a few weeks in the whole span of their married life, when they would conceive the two children now considered sufficient for a family!

"Of course we have now given up the idea that sex exists only for reproduction. We recognize that it is an expression of love, and we don't hesitate to control its reproductive function.

"A third aspect of sex morality among some medieval religionists was to consider it wicked to *enjoy* sex. Married couples were sometimes told that they were permitted to have intercourse if it was their deliberate intention to have a child, and that they must focus their minds calmly on that. But if for a moment they found themselves *enjoying* the experience, they were committing sin! Of course, this was absurd, because in fact it is sexual desire that makes sexual functioning possible!

"I have no doubt that these rules were made sincerely by men (I don't think women were ever consulted) who believed they were doing right. But they simply didn't know the facts about human sexuality. With increased enlightenment, people are changing their views and behavior.

"Now for a more difficult subject. We generally agree that married people may relieve their accumulating sexual tensions, and enjoy meeting each other's sexual needs, while cutting off the reproductive aspects of sex by the use of contraceptives. But what about the unmarried? What recourse do they have?

"We're all sexual beings, and all have sex drives. Even people who never express sex physically in any recognizable way are found to show evidence of sexual interest. If their mental and emotional life is examined, including their dreams, these facts emerge. You can't really divide people into two classes—the sexual, who get married, and the sexless, who don't.

"So what about the unmarried? Can they be expected to shut off sex merely by exercising self-control? A few celibate priests and nuns, very strongly motivated, may have achieved this by heroic effort, though we now know that even some of them have severe problems. But the great majority of unmarried people, in their years of health and vigor, have strong and recurring sexual needs; and the testimony of all the studies that have been made is that they meet these needs in one way or another.

"The Kinsey studies, first published in 1948, opened many eyes—and shocked many people. Kinsey talked about 'sexual outlets,' and we should now look at some of these. The simplest one, readily available at all times, is masturbation, or self-stimulation. As recently as the early years of this century, this was the subject of dire warnings to young men (it was perhaps not known at that time that young women masturbate too). They were threatened with all kinds of dreadful consequences to health and life, from blindness to insanity, if they persisted in this practice. These warnings came not only from clergymen, but from doctors too, although there was no medical evidence to support them.

"Nowadays, we know that masturbation is completely harmless, physically and mentally. It may be disturbing emotionally if you *believe* it is doing you harm, just as you can feel very ill if you are only suffering from indigestion but believe you're having a heart attack.

"Another 'outlet' Kinsey called 'petting to climax.' This takes place between a man and woman when they mutually decide that sexual intercourse wouldn't be appropriate. Usually they are not married; but there are times in married life when this can conveniently be a substitute for intercourse. We know that many couples use this as a form of premarital sex because it avoids any risk of pregnancy.

"Next we come to sexual intercourse before or outside marriage. The major objection to this has always been the possibility of pregnancy. Contraceptives have reduced this risk, though there is no 100% sure method. Presumably, now that abortion is legally and readily available, more people will dare to risk pregnancy. As a scientist, of course, I see another objection to intercourse outside marriage—the possibility of catching venereal disease.

"Our modern knowledge makes it necessary for us to re-examine many of our earlier judgments. Take homosexuality as an example. (Incidentally, here your pastor and I differ rather strongly.) We now know that certain people grow up to be attracted to their own sex rather than to the other. For them, bodily contacts between persons of the same sex are not at all disgusting, but are expressions of love. These people don't *choose* to feel that way. It is believed that their sexual orientation is the result of completely unconscious factors in their early conditioning. In other words, what is abnormal for the rest of us is normal for them. In our culture, these homosexually inclined people one day woke up to the fact of being different, that their desires were not the same as other people's. They then had to work out a way to handle this difference. Some seek and receive professional help, for while many psychiatrists no longer consider homosexuality pathological (that is, a sickness), this is by no means a universal opinion among them. They are still studying the matter, as I know the churches are.

"Meanwhile, laws have been changing, with the Scandinavian countries and Britain leading the way. The trend today is to regard homosexual acts which take place in private, between consenting adults, as entirely legal. This has led to a demand, on the part of some homosexuals, for marriage between persons of the same sex to be recognized. A few such marriages have already been performed. Of course such unions can't produce children. But since we believe today that marriage is not just for procreation, but for love and companionship, the question we have to face is—'If marriage between a man and woman who have no children, but who love each other, is acceptable, why not also marriage between a man and a man, or a woman and a woman, who love each other?'"

Dr. Franklin here pauses, and Pastor Russell comes forward.

"We decided in advance that I would interject a few thoughts here, for Dr. Franklin and I disagree. I don't despise homosexuals, but at the same time I can't accept their behavior as fitting into the realm of what I believe to be normal behavioral patterns.

"While many laws arose in the Old Testament because of cultural attitudes, there were always extremely strong injunctions against homosexuality. God uses the word 'abomination' to describe such acts. You can find clear examples of this in Leviticus 18 and 20. The attitude in the New Testament is even more adamant. You have only to read Romans 1 (especially verses 26–27) to see how strongly Paul speaks against such actions. In 1 Corinthians 6 he does so again.

"For my part, I hope I would never despise or reject homosexuals as persons, but as a Christian I find it difficult to think of their behavior as acceptable and blessed by God."

A hand is raised near the back.

"Dr. Russell, I don't agree with you at all! I am sure there are many fine Christians who are not heterosexuals. They are different from what you describe as the norm—so you condemn them?"

"No, I don't condemn *them*, but I personally can't agree with their actions. But let me say this also, I don't believe in adultery. Or lying. Or stealing. Or gossiping. But I don't reject any person for doing these things. I don't agree with their actions. I tell them so, as the occasion is appropriate. But I also endeavor to love and help them."

"I still don't agree with you, Dr. Russell. And perhaps you and I could talk when the others go into the small groups."

"Fine. Now, back to Dr. Franklin."

"Thank you. Dr. Russell and I do disagree. That's all right. We can accept that in each other. Just as Dr. Russell has the right to disagree with me, so have you. However, it is my sincere opinion that our modern generation does not, by and large, hold such a restrictive view. In looking at what is right and what is wrong in sexual behavior, they base their judgments on human values.

"I'll close by trying to explain what I mean by the term 'human values.' First, responsible people never have the right to use sex in any way that would hurt or exploit another. You can say this in different words if you like. Perhaps it comes out easier for you to say that sexual acts between people should always express friendly or loving relationships.

"This cuts across the old Victorian concepts which implied that as long as sex was confined to marriage, it was always right. In terms of human values, sex could be, and often is, wrongly used between marriage partners. Sex should never be treated as a reward for the mate nor held back as a punishment. But then, as Dr. Russell pointed out to me in our private discussions, even the apostle Paul argued for that point! You'll find his statement in 1 Corinthians 7:5.

"Second, human values, if upheld, would not result in bringing an unwanted or unloved child into the world. For married couples and for some unmarried, too, this places upon them great responsibilities.

"Third, sexual acts which are harmful to good family life, or destructive to the social order, are irresponsible.

"I have run over my time, and I know you may want to ask questions."

III

"We thank you, Dr. Franklin, for your frank statement. Rethinking our Christian sex morality isn't going to be easy, but we must try to face up to it. Now the meeting is open for questions."

"Dr. Franklin, what should we parents do about the sex education of our children?"

"That's a big question, and I'll try to give you a short answer. It depends on what you mean by sex education. To me, it means giving people the facts and encouraging them to examine human values as guidelines for sexual behavior. But some religious people oppose this, because it seems to open the minds of youngsters to facts which can't be squared with the traditional beliefs. What those people want is not for their children to be *educated* about sex, but *indoctrinated* in the traditional attitudes. You see, the two things are very different. You have to decide which you want for your children, and then do what seems appropriate."

"Another question?"

"Dr. Franklin, don't you think new attitudes to sex have led to an awful lot of harm? Wouldn't we be better back in the old days?"

"I agree that many people have been hurt by sexual freedom. But my guess is that at least as much and possibly more suffering resulted from the older system. Everything is out in the open now, and the mass media publicize all the excesses and abuses. Formerly, rigid attitudes to sex caused a vast amount of human misery, but it was all hidden and hushed up. Documented accounts first came into public knowledge from Freud's records of his patients in Vienna. Others soon presented similar documentation. I think the excesses practiced in recent years represent only a reaction to the long years of suppression, and will not continue."

"Thank you again, Dr. Franklin. I wish we had more time for questions. You may bring them up in your groups and discuss them there. I don't think I need take up further time in suggesting topics for you to discuss. This is a highly controversial subject, and one which Christians will go on discussing for a long time."

Genesis 2:24
Leviticus 18:22; 20:13
Matthew 19:5–6
Romans 1:24–32
1 Corinthians 5:1–5; 6:9–20; 7:5–9
Ephesians 5:31
1 Timothy 4:1–4
Hebrews 13:4

Chapter 5

Love

"WELCOME TO THE FIFTH SESSION of our course on 'Men, Women, and God: Families Today and Tomorrow.' Our subject for this evening is Love.

"One Sunday, when Thomas Carlyle, the great Scottish writer, returned home from morning worship, his wife asked him what the sermon had been about. 'Love,' was Carlyle's reply. 'And what was it like?' asked his wife. 'Well,' said Carlyle, 'it was like a flea struggling in a barrel of molasses.'

"Love is a vast subject, and in our session tonight we may not do any better than the Scottish preacher! However, as in our other sessions, I'm going to have some help. I have invited Dr. Frank Randall, a young faculty member in the Department of Psychology at Fieldstone College, to open up the subject for us.

"Dr. Randall, welcome to our church and to this session."

I

"Thank you, Dr. Russell. I share your feelings about the bigness of the subject, and I'm not sure that *two* fleas in a barrel of molasses are much better than one! However, I'll do my best.

"There are many approaches to this subject. The philosophers discuss love in a detached and theoretical manner. The novelists and the poets write about it to reflect people's living experience of it. Religion has a good deal to say about love, and your pastor can speak from that point of view. What I want to do, as a psychologist, is to consider how we all develop our capacity for love in the process of our growth to maturity. I understand that you want a non-technical presentation of the subject, and that you are interested especially in love between men and women, and in family relationships.

"Havelock Ellis once said, 'To live is to love, and to love is to live.' He didn't mean that this happened automatically, but that this is what *should* happen, that the meaning of maturity is to become a loving person. So let's look at the stages through which we pass as we grow to maturity. I'm going to refer to seven of them.

"First is the achievement of *self-love*. This normally occurs in the first year of infancy. Studies of babies show that, if they are loved and cared for, they develop a sense of worth which makes them happy and comfortable. Deprived infants who don't have this experience may actually sicken and die; or they may grow up to be insecure, disturbed adults. We have reason to believe that until you love yourself you can't really love anyone else.

"The second stage is when children achieve *object love*, and the initial love object is the mother. At first they take all that their mothers do for them for granted. They then become aware that mothers can give or withhold the satisfactions they want, and that if they behave in ways that are pleasing to her, things work out better. They make the effort to please her and find a sense of power and joy in being able to do so. At this stage, children are really prompted by self-interest, but derive a sense of happiness and security from the relationship—the close bodily contact, the feeling of being cared for, the satisfaction of giving pleasure. All these contribute to their later love lives.

"Third, they develop love for other members of the family—father, brothers, sisters. As children develop they realize they can't continue to be in the center of the picture. They have to consider the interests of others. This is hard, and they may fight it. But in healthy families, children learn to find satisfaction in give-and-take relationships. This is what we call the process of *socialization*, and it usually begins in the kinship group.

"The fourth stage occurs gradually through the *friendships* children make outside the family circle, with neighborhood peers and schoolmates. Now they are no longer privileged persons; they're just part of the group. A special aspect of this stage of development comes in late childhood, when children form close gangs made up of members of their own sex. Often these gangs closely resemble primitive tribes, with deep attachments among the members. All outsiders are rigidly excluded—the 'in-group' as compared to the 'out-group,' in sociological language.

"The fifth stage comes with *sexual awakening.* The awakening of strong sex drives at puberty throws the developing personality off balance. The power of sexual desire makes the boy uncertain and embarrassed in the presence of an attractive girl, and at first he wants to keep her at a distance. The girl in turn avows disgust toward boys.

"But then a secret interest in the other sex begins to develop. This is marked by attempts to attract their attention, but in a way by which either can disclaim any responsibility for the attempt. For example, a boy, turning a corner and seeing several girls, immediately begins a series of acrobatics—obviously to attract their attention. He can deny this motive to himself by saying he just felt like some exercise. The girls giggle as he goes past—also obviously to attract his attention. The boy tends to begin his advances with teasing and horseplay. The girls object vociferously but want it.

"Even when boys and girls begin pairing off at this stage, their attraction for each other is usually very diffused. When feelings of romantic love develop, they are either not responded to, or, if they are mutual, they are short-lived—though there is also considerable heartbreak when they terminate. Neither the boy nor the girl is ready for depth relationships with one individual. They solve the problem by switching from one to another.

"The sixth stage follows later, and we can use Havelock Ellis' term *monoerotic* to describe it. As the girl and the boy gain experience in being with each other, their diffused feeling of attraction to the opposite sex gradually focuses on a particular choice, and they enter into a relationship of some depth. They may even feel ready to marry. Both become able to combine into one special relationship all previous learnings about loving—sharing, family loyalty, friendship, and sex attraction.

"The seventh stage is somewhat different from the others, because it can be developing all the time, and because it is never fully completed. It is growth toward what we call *altruism*, which comes from the Latin word *alter*, meaning *the other*. It is the opposite of egoism, the state of being self-centered.

"Marriage is the stage in life at which our growth in altruistic love is put to a severe test, because it can't be a good marriage unless each is able to love the other as much as she loves herself. Later, in parenthood, the test is even more severe, because a young child can't return love in equal measure, so parents have to offer children the kind of love that gives more than it gets.

"Altruism can on occasion go all the way toward complete self-giving. At least this can happen in a major crisis. For example, in Dickens' *Tale of Two Cities*, Sidney Carton, out of love for Lucy Manette, dies on the guillotine so that his lookalike may escape to England and marry Lucy. But as a way of life, in continuing relationships, it's doubtful whether complete altruism is either possible or advisable. There are egotistic people who exploit the self-giving of others, and it contributes nothing to their growth to be able to get away with it. In a healthy family, the members give and get in roughly equal proportions. I think people can be considered to be pretty mature when they enjoy giving to others as much as they enjoy getting.

"There's one other thing I'd like to add. I have roughly sketched out seven stages we pass through as we grow in the capacity to love. Unfortunately, this doesn't happen to all of us. Our growth can become arrested at any one of these stages. The word we psychologists use for this arrest in growth is 'fixation.' We get 'stuck' at one particular stage and don't move on any further.

"Let me very briefly go back over the seven stages and refer to the possible fixations. As I have already said, the people who never achieve self-love are in serious trouble and never learn to relate significantly to others. Children who never personalize their relationship to love objects throughout their lives treat all other persons as objects to be manipulated in their own self-interests. People who don't experience proper socialization in their families spend their lives trying to make themselves the center of the picture, through money or fame or other means. Those who can't manage their sex drives toward the opposite sex usually don't marry, and some may develop into practicing homosexuals. The person who doesn't progress beyond the polyerotic stage may only seek to exploit the opposite sex, unable to enter into a depth relationship with a chosen mate. The person who fails to develop an adequate capacity for altruistic love always tends to use relationships to gain personal advantages.

"In closing I confess I've tried to cover a lot of ground and have oversimplified many processes that are really much more complex than I have made them appear to be. So please regard what I've said as a rough sketch."

"Dr. Randall, you've been very helpful with your presentation.

II

"As I try now to relate all this to Christian teaching, I begin with the now familiar Greek word *agape*, used in the New Testament to describe the special kind of love that is expected of Christian believers.

"It has been said that 'love' is the most overworked four-letter word in the English language. The Greeks were better off, because they had three different words. These three words are worth looking at, because they help us to identify the different kinds of love, or at least the three components of love which Dr. Randall has described as they appear in the process of personality development.

"The first word is *eros*, which you can recognize in our own word *erotic*, or sexual love. This Greek word could be roughly translated as *desire*. Sexual love is of course based on desire, and some people think that sex really has nothing to do with love. However, desire is probably present in all love and should be recognized as a part of love. But if love is *only* desire, it will prove to be rather fickle, because it disappears when desire has been satisfied.

"The second Greek word is *philia*. It means friendship love, which is based on common interests and a feeling of mutual liking. This is more durable than *eros*; but it can fail, because it is based on liking. People who like each other can fall into disagreement and hostility.

"The third Greek word is *agape*, which I have already mentioned; and this means something stronger and deeper. It has many shades of meaning, but basically in the Bible it describes love not based on the loved one's actions or worth. God's love is of this kind—not based on our goodness or our past, present, or future actions. This love was shown in the selection of the Hebrew nation:

> It was not because you were more in number than any other people that the LORD set his love upon you and chose you, for you were the fewest of all peoples; but it is because the LORD loves you . . . .

In the New Testament it is best illustrated in Romans 5:8: 'But God shows his love for us in that while we were yet sinners, Christ died for us.' We human beings are recipients of God's love, and yet there is nothing we have done which deserves or earns it.

"This *agape* involves the will and is not a mere emotion. So when we love others as God has first loved us, we recognize that it is our duty to stand with them, whether or not we have any particular feelings of liking them, whether or not they 'deserve' it.

"If we apply this to love between members of a family, we can see what a strong, enduring bond it forms. A husband continues loving his wife even when she temporarily exasperates him, and she does the same. Parents don't stop loving when their children behave badly or let them down. Children continue loving parents even when parents punish them or frustrate their wishes.

"I believe we can apply these ideas to many of the situations Dr. Randall talked about. True self-love is really what we call self-esteem, a feeling of our own worth. Jesus' second great commandment, as found in Matthew 22, says, 'You shall love your neighbor *as yourself*,' implying that you *can't* truly love your neighbor if you don't already love yourself.

"The mother's devotion to her children makes them realize they are truly loved. They become convinced that they are therefore lovable people. Children's love for their mother moves to a higher level when they pass the stage of regarding her as a kind of servant who comes when they cry. They get to know her as a person and love her for what she is rather than merely for what she does.

"Friendship grows deeper when two people move from just liking each other's company to admiring and respecting each other as persons. Romantic love, based on sexual desire, grows into what we call conjugal love when boy and girl not only want to enjoy each other, but want to make personal sacrifices to further each other's growth and well-being. Unless *agape* takes over, however, and provides the effort needed to go on encouraging the development of that potential, romantic love soon withers and dies.

"A fundamental message of Christianity is love, God's love and then our love in response. As 1 John says, 'We love, because he first loved us.' Our problem is that all too often we don't seem to manage to put this into practice in our daily living and in our family relationships. If we profess that all people should live together in harmony, yet can't even live together in love with those nearest and dearest to us, our message to the world is going to sound a little unconvincing. I believe this is a problem most of us share, and we need all the help we can give one another in solving it.

III

"Well, my time is up. At this point I'll give you a chance to ask questions."

"Pastor, you talked about love as if it was a duty. I always thought love was—well, something a person *felt*. Can you make your feelings change?"

"Yes, I did talk about the duty to love. I believe we make a mistake in stressing *feelings* of love, forgetting that we can perform loving acts even if, as the moment, we aren't *feeling* very loving. Sometimes young people get the idea that a marriage is doomed when the two people no longer feel affectionate toward each other. But loving feelings can return, and one way to help them return is to act deliberately as if we really felt loving.

"I remember a story about an elevator operator who was whistling one morning, and someone said, 'Sam, you must feel cheerful today.' 'No sir,' said Sam, 'I'm not whistling because I *feel* cheerful. I'm whistling because I hope it will *make* me feel cheerful.' Love is a matter of the will as well as of the emotions."

"I'd like to ask Dr. Randall about fixations. How do they happen? Can they be cured?"

"Fixation means the arrest of one or more phases of development at a childhood or adolescent level. Normally we develop progressively in all respects—intellectually, emotionally, socially, sexually. Even though this process is not always a smooth one, our personality grows as a whole, and we become increasingly capable of meeting different types of situations. But in some cases an individual fails to develop in one major respect. This feature of personality remains 'fixated' at some early stage.

"Fixations may occur at any stage of child development. A girl may remain so emotionally dependent on her mother that she feels uncomfortable without her and won't enter school when the time comes. Persistent baby talk, thumb-sucking, and temper tantrums are further symptoms of early fixation.

"Or sexual development may be blocked. A growing boy may be so firmly fixed at the stage of masturbation that he cannot establish relationships with the opposite sex.

"*Why* do fixations occur? There are undoubtedly many possible causes, and sometimes several may operate at once. Some parents consciously or unconsciously encourage their children to remain at an immature stage of development because it is 'cute' or because they don't want to feel that the children—or they themselves—are growing older. Such parents keep their children dependent on them and give them too little practice in independent thought and action. It has also been found that children who are overcriticized or overprotected frequently feel too insecure to venture into more mature behavior. Others fail to develop in one or more of the stages because they meet failure at play or in school. Parents may also instill active fear, disgust, or guilt feelings in the sexual sphere which inhibit development there.

"In short, fixations produce immature, defective character traits and special vulnerability in the areas where the individual has failed to develop.

"As to the cure, psychotherapy seems to offer the best chance for professional help. Therapists become parent figures, trying to help fixated persons go back emotionally to the place where fixation occurred and make a more healthy adjustment. This is a long, difficult, and costly procedure. If the damage was done early in life, it may be impossible to make it good.

"This doesn't mean that everything must be left up to the professionals. Individuals need love and acceptance. You may not be able to help people with severe problems, but many respond to caring, and concern for others is one of the good examples of altruistic love."

"Dr. Russell, both of you said a lot about self-love. But now I'm confused. Jesus said that if people wanted to be disciples, they had to deny themselves. I thought self-renunciation was what we had to do."

"I'll try to tackle that one. I know this can be confusing. I find it helpful, though, to remember that in a sense we have several selves. We have a lower self, which seeks things inappropriate to our good and to the good of others, and we have a higher self.

"Our task is to recognize our actions and become aware of them. We need to believe in what we properly term 'our best selves' and firmly deal with the demands of the less respectable parts of our nature.

"To renounce the self totally would be impossible. At the level of personality, that would be committing suicide. But Jesus did say in the Sermon on the Mount that if your right eye causes you to sin, pluck it out and throw it away. He didn't mean than literally. He meant that if your lower nature keeps turning your gaze in the wrong direction, you must renounce the part of yourself that was prompting you toward wrong action. So while we love ourselves as worthwhile persons, we dislike our unworthy impulses.

"But friends, our time has gone. We've had a lively discussion of a very important subject. We two fleas have struggled for a while in that barrel of molasses. Now it's your turn to get in!"

(Blackboard verses)
Deuteronomy 7:7–8
Psalm 103
Matthew 5:29, 43–48; 22:37–40
Mark 8:34
John 15:12–17
Romans 5:8
Philippians 2:1–4
Colossians 3:12–17
1 John 4:7–21

Chapter 6

Family Relationships

"OUR SUBJECT FOR TONIGHT is family relationships. This should help us review some of the insights we have gained in our earlier sessions, as we consider what it takes to enable family members to live happily together.

"Our visiting expert tonight is Dr. Norman Belgrave, a former Methodist pastor who is now a full-time marriage and family counselor. In discussing tonight's session, Dr. Belgrave and I decided it would be best for me to go first. I want us to take a look at families in the Bible so that we may understand how different they were from the families of today. I'll repeat some things I've said before, so this can be a sort of summary of what the Bible tells us about family relationships.

I

"We have to remember that the people who lived in Palestine in Bible times lived a very simple life compared with ours. Of course there were no movies, no radio or TV, no newspapers, magazines, or books. There was no electricity or gas, no automobiles, railroads, or airplanes—not even bicycles. Cities were few, and very different from our own. Homes had no refrigerators, sinks, or toilets, no glass or screens in the windows. There were no stores or banks or hospitals as we know them. The list could go on and on, but I hope I've said enough to make my point.

"While no one pattern applied to all, most families lived in very simple homes in small villages. It was an agricultural community—they raised crops, and had flocks of sheep and goats. The children helped their parents—they fetched water from the well, gathered firewood, worked in the home and on the land, and took care of the animals.

"The education of children was ordinarily the responsibility of parents. Mothers taught their daughters to be good housewives—cleaning, preparing food, making clothes, tending the oil lamps, raising the younger children. Fathers took over the training of their sons—preparing the land, sowing the seed, gathering in the harvest, watching over the animals, driving off wild beasts, buying and selling, rendering first aid, fixing broken tools. And especially important, boys and girls learned to observe the family religious rituals.

"Thus parents and children were together a great deal. But familiarity was not encouraged. Parents exercised authority over their children and complete obedience was expected. The father had absolute power. He could impose harsh punishments. He could even sell his children or put them to death. Abraham was ready to offer up his son Isaac as a sacrifice; Jephthah the judge apparently either put his daughter to death or assigned her to a state of perpetual virginity. So children learned, above everything else, to honor their parents and obey them.

"But in spite of the complete parental authority, there appears to have been plenty of love and tenderness. Children were valued as gifts of God, and Old Testament and New speak of parental responsibility and care in no uncertain terms.

"What about husbands and wives? Hebrew boys and girls were usually married soon after puberty. Their parents probably picked their partners for them, although romantic attachments were not unknown. The husband was the boss, and his wife's role was a submissive one. A man viewed his wife first as the mother of the children he very much desired. Childlessness was a terrible tragedy—recall Rachel or Hannah or Elizabeth, mother of John the Baptist. Sex was considered something good, to be enjoyed by both husband and wife. Thus Paul the apostle, who has often been accused of being prudish, said very clearly in 1 Corinthians 7 that married couples musn't defraud one another by withholding sexual fulfillment.

"Companionship in marriage was not forgotten. In the creation

51

story, God made woman because it was not good for the man to be alone. The unitive function of sex, the two becoming one, was recognized as well as its reproductive function.

"Bible references congratulate the husband who is fortunate enough to have a good wife, and commiserate with the poor guy who has a bad one.

"There must have been conflicts and quarrels in Bible families, although this isn't so likely to happen where there is a recognized power structure—husband over wife, parent over child, elder child over younger child. But in practice such a structure doesn't always prevail. Certainly conflict seems to have developed, often in the form of sibling rivalry, as in the very first family, when Cain killed his brother Abel. Sibling rivalry is also seen in the stories of Jacob and Esau, Joseph, and the prodigal son.

"Family life has become more complicated since Biblical times, because human society itself has become more complicated. Most families now live in complex urban settings. They face a pluralistic culture, where children are exposed to a diversity of influences besides their home training. Our families tend to be more democratic, less authoritarian. Children and young people have rights and opportunities that were quite unknown in the past. They have to make choices, and to take responsibility for their choices, to an extent that would be bewildering to children in simpler cultures. Things are so different that to many the Bible seems irrelevant to family life today.

"Yet in spite of the immense differences, the basic teaching of the Bible about human relationships is as valid today as it ever was—the call to respect every individual as a child of God, to be honest and straightforward in all our dealings, and to recognize our mutual need for love and sympathy and support from the 'significant others' in our lives. Not just Proverbs but the Gospels and the New Testament letters too are full of wise advice about human relationships. It could be an interesting project to go through the New Testament and collect references which apply to the interactions between family members.

II

"But that must be left for another time. Now I want to introduce our guest speaker, Dr. Belgrave. He will speak to us about family relationships in our contemporary society."

"I certainly appreciate your invitation. As Pastor Russell told you, I was formerly a Methodist pastor. I went into marriage and family counseling not to leave the church, but to get into a more specialized ministry. I feel very much at home with you in this excellent program you have set up.

"Pastor Russell has pointed out the great differences between families in the Bible and families today. One interesting aspect is that when we Christians in the West study the older cultures of our world we find that the family life of those cultures is much more like that of Bible times than family life in the newer nations such as our own. When you consider how families are breaking down today, it's very difficult to decide whether our family relationships in so-called Christian countries are more Christian or less Christian than those of so-called heathen lands.

"However, we can't put the clock back, so we must do the best we can to improve our family relationships where we are, and that's what I want to talk to you about.

"If family relationships are more difficult to manage successfully today, this is offset to some extent by the fact that we *understand* what we call the dynamics of interpersonal relations better now than ever before. Personally, I feel somewhat optimistic about what we can do to help families function better, once we have a chance to put our knowledge into action.

"As your pastor has pointed out, we have moved family relationships toward a democratic pattern—everyone has a voice in family affairs. That sounds great. Democracy is a wonderful idea. But don't forget, it's also very difficult to put into operation. Look at the efforts to encourage democracies in developing countries in Asia and Africa. Nearly all of them have collapsed and been replaced by dictatorships of one kind or another. Why? One reason is that democracy in principle makes everyone equal. When we are all equal we all want to be heard, we all want a voice in decision making. Obviously this can lead to great confusion and disorder, and we may finally reach the point where it seems better to let a strong individual take over and make the decisions for us.

"Similar troubles have occurred in the modern family. When in democratic families we recognize the equality of all, real complications sometimes result. When wife and husband have equal votes, what do they do when one votes on each side? When the child has a right to question a parent's judgment, how do they settle the matter?

"When we allow differences of opinion to be expressed, we inevitably have disagreement. When disagreements are expressed, conflict results; points of view are argued with increasing vigor and accompanied by stronger and stronger emotions. This goes on a great deal of the time in modern families. In the old pattern, the matter would have been swiftly settled. Whoever was in authority announced his or her judgment, and no more discussion was necessary.

"What I'm saying is that conflict becomes inevitable in democratic family relationships. Some Christians feel this should not be so. They feel that anger and disagreement have no place in a Christian family and that peace should reign. So what do they do? They swallow their hostile feelings and suppress their disagreements. This is like putting the garbage in a closet and thinking you're rid of it. Beneath the surface, the anger still smolders, ill feelings rankle, a sense of injustice stings. The result is that relationships that should be warm and affectionate become cold and formal.

"If we're going to have meaningful family relationships, we have to bring the issues, and the feelings about the issues, out into the open, and work at resolving them. This needs to be done again and again. Facing up to differences and dealing with those differences is necessary in order to live together in a modern democratic family. Healthy families are *not* families where conflict is absent. They are families which have learned to deal with conflict and to try to cooperate as equals.

"Husband and wife must set the pattern. We can't have a really wholesome family without a functional marriage at its center. Marriage is the nucleus of the family, the foundation-stone on which it rests. So married couples need skills in dealing with conflict. How can parents help their children to resolve their differences, if they as husband and wife aren't willing to work out their own?

"Once marriage partners have learned to deal with their own conflicts, they can better handle the conflicts that arise between them and their children. This isn't easy, but it is possible. The generation gap presents a real problem, especially when the children get into their teens. But although we hear shrill cries of anguish from many parents who are failing to relate to their children, there are plenty of other parents quietly getting on with the job and making a success of it.

"Parents often find it difficult to remember how it feels to be a child. Even if they *can* remember, it doesn't always help, because children today feel so differently. So the parents simply have to *listen* to their children; otherwise they can't know what's going on. That means keeping the lines of communication open. I'll have more to say about communication later.

"What about discipline? The old heavy-handed approaches of the authoritarian system have very poor chances of succeeding today. It is to be hoped that more parents will adopt the cooperative system of discipline, wherein the parent says to the child—'My job is not to give you orders, but to help you manage your own life, make your own decisions, and stand on your own feet. I'm also responsible to God for you, and want to protect you from the dangerous situations you may get into because of your lack of experience. I'll give you freedom and responsibility a little at a time, as we both feel you're ready for it. If you can handle it, then you've earned the right to a little more freedom. If you can't, then we'll wait until you've gained enough new experience to try again.' Once this kind of agreement is established between parent and child, the way is open for cooperation. Without such an understanding, they're only going to fight each other.

"What about sibling relationships? I was interested in what your pastor said about siblings in Bible times, and I think he may be right. After all, those kids in restricted families couldn't express any hostility to their parents or other elders, so they took it out on one another. Also, while husband and wife choose one another, siblings don't, and you often find some pretty severe personality clashes. However, I suspect siblings get along better with each other nowadays, because they gang up in their common opposition to adults!

"If husband and wife can manage their relationships responsibly and parents and children manage theirs, the general atmosphere should be conducive to healthy sibling relationships. And research indicates that siblings who compete vigorously at some stages in their development often enjoy close relationships later on. This suggests that a certain amount of sibling rivalry provides useful learning experiences.

"I now want to say something about the all-important question of communication. In recent years there have been some new studies in family communication.

"In many families there appears to be much more negative communication than positive. As a general rule, when we feel angry at another family member we express it, but when we have warm feelings we tend to keep them to ourselves! This doesn't make sense. A British psychologist, Ian Suttie, talked about a 'taboo on tenderness' in our culture to describe the difficulty some of us have in expressing feelings of affection to each other.

"To remedy this, efforts are being made to train family members—husbands and wives, parents and children—to communicate better with each other. The results have been encouraging. Members of a family live so close together that unless they can share their feelings with each other, misunderstandings and tensions tend to develop. But when they are open about their feelings, both positive and negative, there is usually a marked improvement in their relationship. It has been found that when they merely attack each other, little or no progress is made in resolving conflict. But when they share hurt feelings, without attacking each other or defending themselves, this often opens up the way to resolving the difficulty.

"The central issue, of course, is what to do with anger. Some people bottle it up and allow it to simmer. Others explode and get relief—often at the expense of someone else. Expressing anger is healthier than suppressing it. But there is an even better way: acknowledge anger; regard it as your personal problem; and ask the person at whom you're angry to help you handle it. This approach can lead to constructive results.

"To sum up, family relationships are more difficult today, because of our insistence on equality, than they have ever been before. But we are learning new methods of dealing with conflict. Where these methods are understood and used effectively, families enjoy warmer and closer relationships than ever before."

III

"Thank you, Norman, for being so helpful—and so hopeful too. Now I'm sure there are questions."

"Pastor, you seemed to me to suggest that the Bible isn't a good guide for family behavior. Is that what you really think?"

"I believe that the great principles taught in the Bible are the best of all guides to human behavior. But I think the ways in which people behaved in Palestine two or three thousand years ago don't necessarily provide a pattern we can just duplicate for our life today. For example, most of us eat pork and tuna today, but according to Old Testament dietary laws, they were forbidden. But I *do* believe the Bible can show us, better than any other source, how to live in love and harmony with God and people. The principles don't change; but the *application* of the principles has to be adjusted to our particular living conditions."

"I'd like to ask Dr. Belgrave what parents can do to change their system of discipline if they decide they've been on the wrong track."

"I suppose you mean, how can they switch from the authoritarian system to the cooperative? First, both parents begin with a change of attitude, because if one works one system and the other another, the result will be chaos! When they have both decided to change, they call a family conference and discuss the change in pattern with the children. Remember that the new system is based on *cooperation*. It won't work until children clearly understand what's going on and agree with it.

"This a quite a venture to make, so everyone must be ready to make it succeed. It just doesn't work if we switch back to the old heavy-handed methods as soon as things get difficult. You can't mix the two systems—you must choose one or the other. Even a poor system of discipline, if *consistently applied*, is better than off-again, on-again experiments with a good system. At least in the authoritarian relationships, everyone knew the rules."

"Pastor, I've been listening to you talk about this democratic or cooperative method. At first it sounded awfully good to me. But as I've been thinking more about it, it's a little frightening. What if my twelve-year-old daughter insists on making decisions that I, because I've lived longer and experienced more, can see are clearly wrong? Or my five-year-old Tommy? He's quite immature."

"First, Martha, you have to take a few chances. We've tried to point out that it's not easy. You may have setbacks and run into difficulties, but we feel it's worth the risk.

"Second, the cooperative method does not mean a complete abdication of your responsibility and authority. As parents we are concerned for the maturing of our children. Our discipline is to help them become stable, healthy adults. By giving them responsibility and freedom over a course of time, we train them for independence.

"The third thing I want to say is that the cooperative method is *not* anarchy—where every member does as he or she chooses! This method aims at open discussion of problems, possible solutions, and guidance toward resolving them. Rather than dictate, parents guide and suggest alternatives. Children have their chances to speak up—and it's important that they be thoroughly heard."

"Excuse me for interrupting, pastor, but my wife and I hit upon something like this a couple of years ago. We're sold on it. It's like training children to make their decisions about careers, or clothes, or kinds of recreation. We offer our ideas and try to help, but we're teaching our children to make decisions themselves and to know that, once they put those decisions into action, they are responsible. We don't regret this. I think it's brought our family a lot closer together. My children know—perhaps better than before—that I love them. They know my wife and I will listen."

IV

"Great. I'm sure others have similar contributions to make, so let's move into small groups. We've raised plenty of questions for you to consider. It might be a good idea, though, to focus on your own families. How do you settle disagreements at home? How do you handle anger when it arises? What system of discipline has been found to work best? How well do you manage to communicate your real feelings to each other, and to accept each other's real feelings—the affirmative ones as well as the bad? How well do the parents understand and identify with their children? How well do the children understand and identify with their parents? Let's try to get into some of these issues together."

(Verses for blackboard)
Genesis 2:18–24; 4:1–8; 22:1–14; 25:29–34; 27:1–41; 30:1; 37:3–5
Leviticus 11:7–8, 10–12
Judges 11
1 Samuel 1
Luke 1:7, 13; 15:25–32
1 Corinthians 7:5

Chapter 7

The Family & the Community

Item from Church Bulletin
First Presbyterian Church, Setonville, Ohio

THE UNSEASONABLE, INCREDIBLE BLIZZARD earlier this week caused cancellation of the seventh session of the series on family life. Because the planning committee has already lined up leaders for the remaining weeks, we will go ahead on this coming Wednesday to discuss "The Family of the Future."

This represents a major shift in the series, from looking at our basic Christian beliefs about the family to an emphasis on the future. The next five weeks will focus there. What kind of relationships between women and men are likely to develop in the years ahead? Will communes or trial marriages replace the traditional family pattern we've known? Should more children be taken from less than adequate parents and raised by the state? What is women's liberation going to do to our homes?

Come on the next five Wednesday nights to think and talk about these and related concerns. They probably affect your present household; they certainly will affect your children's.

Because of the storm, we missed a key session on the relation of the family to the community around it, which ultimately includes the whole world. Two points need to be remembered: (1) The family must always be aware of the pressures the community puts on it to fragment the home, or to cause it to abandon its values—and, we would say, especially its Christian values. (2) The family has a ministry to the community given it by God, so while it must resist forces that threaten it, it cannot just withdraw. Instead it must at a minimum seek to communicate its spiritual and moral insight to the community, provide youth and adults of Christian integrity to help lead the community, and minister to the whole range of community needs.

We include this paragraph lest in our series we omit this important aspect and seem ingrown and selfish in our concern as Christians for the family in the world of today and tomorrow.

Chapter 8

The Family of the Future

"IN PREVIOUS SESSIONS," begins Pastor Russell, "our focus was on the past and the present. Now we turn to the future, and ask 'Where do we go from here?'

"Tonight we'll have three speakers. Our first is Dr. Mildred Stevenson, Professor of History at Fieldstone College. You may wonder why your committee invited an authority on our human past to speak to us about our human future. We did so because we believe in the continuity of our culture, even though many today are questioning this. Dr. Stevenson, we're eager to hear what you have to tell us."

I

"Thank you, Pastor. None of us can really predict the future of humankind, because there are so many unknown possibilities. All we can do is guess at the directions we may travel if the trends we see now are not interrupted. Since I must be brief, I'll concentrate on three of these trends.

"First, I think we are continuing to move into an international era in which our differences from each other will become less and less important. In the past, differences of race, national loyalty, language, religion, and political ideology have made groups of people enemies to one another. This has led to endless wars and terrible destruction, so that human history has been a continuous record of clashes between rival groups—strong peoples overrunning weaker cultures, only to become eventually soft and weak themselves and to be overrun in turn.

"I believe that a long era of our history is ending at last, especially among the great powers of the world. War has become so sophisticated that it is too dangerous except on a very limited scale. Also, travel, communication, and widespread education are making us realize that human beings are very much alike, and that we must learn to cooperate instead of compete. Hence we've seen a whole structure of international organizations built up, so that instead of fighting one another we can join together to defeat our common enemies—disease, ignorance, poverty, crime, and exploitation.

"The implication is that our traditional cultural differences will cease to divide our human family, as all people everywhere learn to accept one another's pattern of living and values. This will mean that we shall learn to accept and appreciate pluralism—a culture in which people are free to choose their own life-styles. In family life, different patterns will exist side by side, far more than we know it today.

"The second major trend concerns technology. Our lives have been so profoundly changed by the fantastic developments of science that, as Alvin Toffler put it some years ago, we all suffer from 'future shock.' Personally, I think we are now entering a period of reaction from all this. Technology has delivered just about all that we could need to make life pleasant from a material point of view. We are now nearing the saturation point in areas like travel, communication, power, construction, and consumer goods."

Dr. Stevenson chuckles, "But, of course, my grandmother thought that with the invention of radio we had reached the end. I'm only stating that while we'll continue to have *refinements*, technology has nearly reached the end of its work.

"Besides, technological advances have begun to demand a heavy price. Further improvements in the form of material comfort and convenience offer us diminishing returns; they even threaten our environment, health, and happiness. A readjustment of our values is in order. My guess is that it will take the form of a move from the cities back to rural areas; from science back to the arts; from excessive luxury back to comparative simplicity. This trend favors a renewed appreciation of the benefits of home and family life.

"The third trend is linked with the second. Because technology has failed to bring us happiness, I think we are going to shift our emphasis from the improvement of our condition to the improvement of ourselves. We owe a great debt to the natural sciences, but a new era of the behavioral sciences is now about to dawn. The power to make a better life for human beings materially is a mockery if we are unable to enjoy it. What good is it to prolong life for people who are unable to enjoy life? We must give greater attention to the largely neglected area of human potential and the quality of life, to the development of inner creativity. I think this will inevitably focus our attention on the art of human relationships. And I think there could be no better place to begin than with family relationships.

"I don't know what kind of family patterns we'll have in the future. I see little prospect for continuing relationships that make people miserable and are sustained only out of a sense of duty. The emphasis will be on the *quality* of relationships—their power to be creative and fulfilling to those concerned."

II

"Thank you, Dr. Stevenson. Our next speaker is an old friend, family counselor Norman Belgrave, who will tell us how he sees the future of the family. Norman, we're glad to have you with us again."

"I appreciate the opportunity to go into some detail about what families might be like in that new world Dr. Stevenson envisions. The obvious place to begin is with marriage.

"I agree with Dr. Stevenson that families in the future will emphasize the quality of the relationships they make possible. In the past the family fulfilled all kinds of practical functions like providing protection from danger, providing economic security, and educating the new generation. Almost all these needs are now being met outside the family. But our deepest needs, which our complex, impersonal world is less and less able to meet, are for emotional security, a sense of identity and worth, and the opportunity to fulfill ourselves through love, affection, and intimacy.

"The closest and most intimate relationship of all is realized in marriage. A marriage relationship of deep love and trust offers a close companionship in which you feel accepted and esteemed. Because of that security, you can face the adventures and hazards of the outside world with confidence. I believe this is what most people want and need. There are some, I admit, who don't wish to marry or who can't tolerate that kind of closeness, but I believe that now and in the future, marriage can be a really rich and deeply satisfying experience for the majority of people.

"But achieving that kind of relationship isn't easy. The fact is, it's very, very difficult. But some couples do experience it already. Our hope is that it will be increasingly possible for us to enable more and more people to achieve fulfilling relationships in marriage, as we draw on the great advances being made (as Dr. Stevenson reminded us) in the behavioral sciences.

"In that connection, I'm sure the future will see a continuation of our present experiments with varying forms of the man-woman relationship. However, I think you are going to look more closely at these new patterns next week, so I won't say any more now on that subject.

"Let me therefore turn to the future of parenthood. Here too, I think, the emphasis is going to be on quality relationships. Psychotherapy has fairly well documented the fact that the child who has loving parents has the maximum chance to develop into a contented and useful citizen, while the child deprived of loving parents is in danger of growing into a disturbed and maladjusted adult. The implications of this are painful, but we can't afford to go on ignoring them. As someone put it long ago, 'the hand that rocks the cradle rules the world.' We cannot have a truly human society until the people in it are capable of relating in a mature, mutually helpful, and supportive way to each other. Such people are greatly influenced by effective parenting. We cannot forever look to therapists to straighten out what should never have been allowed to go wrong.

"There are those who say the only solution lies in denying the right to have children to those who seem incapable of raising them. That means a program of involuntary sterilization, and it would be an extreme measure. Before we go to such extremes, I trust we'll try the alternative procedure of giving potential parents the opportunity for thorough training for their difficult and responsible task.

"Here as in marriage relationships I hope we'll increasingly make use of the flood of new knowledge which the behavioral sciences are beginning to bring us. For instance, I would like to shift the focus of public education and create schools in which the primary emphasis would be on training for creative relation

64

ships—especially for successful marriage and parenthood.

"Finally, I'll say something about family roles and functions in the future. It seems likely that these will be very different from the past. Families have not moved in the new directions Dr. Stevenson has talked about. Instead, they have often been very conservative institutions, opposing progress in breaking down barriers between religious, national, and racial groups. Great reformers were often opposed by their families and sometimes even disowned by them. We must help families of the future to be more flexible and more open to change."

III

"Thanks, Norman."

"My part in this evening's program is to relate to our Christian values what the other speakers have said. At some points this is simple. At others it may prove to be very difficult.

"First, the simple part. Both speakers have emphasized that the kind of warm, loving intimacy we now find in effective families will be needed more than ever in the future. There is no doubt in my mind that our Christian message puts its central emphasis on love—God's love in Christ shed abroad in human hearts and human lives, and reflected in human relationships at their best. In spite of all the past errors of God's people, Christian culture seems to me to have produced a long line of shining examples of men and women who have risen to great heights in their love for others and in devoted, sacrificial service to the needy. What other world religion has been able to produce equivalent compassion?

"So what we have to offer is just what the world of tomorrow will continue to need for the building of loving families, and I think this is going to be a central emphasis in the churches.

"However, we may have trouble accepting some of the *forms* those families will take. We have grown accustomed to associate Christianity with certain patterns of behavior and certain traditional concepts of the family. These traditions are being vigorously challenged today; and, as both of the previous speakers have suggested, some of the traditions are not going to survive. One significant problem I see is how to distinguish between the letter of the law and the spirit of the law; between what is vital to our Christian message, and what must be given up because it no longer applies to the new world we live in.

"Let me give you some examples. Christians have already had to do a lot of readjusting in their ideas about the relationship between women and men. For instance, we have had to give up the belief that every marriage blessed by the church will turn out to be a truly Christian union and last for a lifetime. We now recognize that a young man and woman can exercise poor judgment and make a mistake in choosing to marry each other. When it is clear that they have failed in their efforts to establish a fulfilling marriage, the charitable thing to do is to release them from their commitment and allow them to go their separate ways. What we do in that instance is to recognize that the inward and spiritual state of the relationship is more important than the outward and visible form of the marriage contract. Such a breaking of contract was unacceptable some years ago, but is this really a departure from Christian principles? I don't think so.

"Here's another example. It was once the understanding of most Christians that married women should meekly obey their husbands in all matters, that their proper place was in the home, and that they shouldn't dabble in business, in politics, or in the affairs of the world outside the home. Likewise, it used to be that young people had to accept the judgments and decisions of their parents in all matters and obey without questioning. Have we really violated Christian principles in moving away from such patterns?

"So it's clear that we've already changed many of our ideas. In the future we may have to change more of them. Again, some examples. It has been a central part of our Christian teaching that sexual intercourse before marriage is a serious sin. Some of us feel reluctant to compromise on this issue. Yet it appears that young people who don't engage in premarital sex are now in a steadily decreasing minority. So what are we to do? Are we to deny church membership or church weddings to young people who have had sex before marriage unless they confess their sinful state and repent? Is this the stand to take?"

"Pastor Russell, your viewpoint disturbs me. Is it right to lower standards just because they're not popular? Right is right, even if no one obeys. I can accept your other examples of how things were in the past, but this one on premarital sex bothers me. It seems to me you're saying that we have to change and say, 'Well, there's nothing we can do to correct the situation, so we'll accept it.' I've always felt that one of the purposes of the church of Jesus Christ is to influence the world by taking a stand, even when it's unpopular.

"Let *me* give an example. I'm thirty years old. I was opposed to the war in Vietnam. I refused to serve in armed combat and my stance was unpopular—in fact, some people right here in our church disagreed and disapproved. But I stood by what I believed. I think that's the way our church ought to be."

"Ronald, you're absolutely right. I do not mean that we ought to lower our standards. I do mean that we need to struggle with the question of morality and the worth of people. I do not approve of premarital sex. But at the same time I want to be open to people—to accept them unconditionally. If I understand my New Testament, that was the attitude of Jesus. He loved people. He accepted them and forgave them. *Then* he said, 'Go and sin no more.'"

"Yes, Pastor, I believe in accepting people, but I think we still have to take a stand on what we believe! Maybe you're saying that, too. It's just that I feel so strongly about influences around us, trying to make us compromise our faith."

"In our small groups I think we will want to discuss this further, but for now let's look at another aspect of this question. Some young people today are cohabiting—living together without being married. Some do this as a way of testing out their relationship before they make a serious commitment to each other, arguing that this is better than getting married, then finding they can't get along together, and getting a divorce. Others say their relationship is permanent and that love holds them together, not a marriage license.

"We may consider this reasoning unsound, but we can hardly call all these young people irresponsible. The church already recognizes non-church marriages that are formally registered by the state. In the Middle Ages, common law marriages were recognized by the Roman Catholic Church, on the reasoning that the couple had taken each other in marriage in the sight of God. How does the church respond to people who now say they have done this and need no religious ceremony?

"We're going to move further into some of these complicated issues in the weeks ahead. All I'm doing now is giving you a foretaste of what's to come! So let's stop and give others besides Ronald time to ask questions."

IV

"Pastor, don't you think we should have more faith in God and let him run the world his way? Take this population question. A Catholic friend of mine says that if we had more people in the world, God would provide them with their daily bread. How would you answer that?"

"I think it depends on the way we believe God works. Some people sincerely believe that God will take care of everything; we only have to trust him. I believe that God's purpose is for us to assume responsibility for our lives, working with him and using the gifts bestowed upon us.

"Why do we have a population problem? Partially because we have used our intelligence to conquer disease and famine, and to lengthen life. We now need to use that same intelligence to control population. I expect God to help me and guide me, but I don't expect him to do for me what I am able to do for myself."

"This question is for Dr. Stevenson. She seems to favor a pluralistic society. But my problem is that in our attempts to live in peace with our non-Christian neighbors, we Christians are always having to compromise our principles, and we could end up with a very weak kind of Christianity."

"I'm very sympathetic toward that problem. It's quite true that tolerating the standards of our neighbors does tend to weaken our own convictions. That's why religious groups in the past have tended either to live apart in segregated communities, or to work hard to convert their neighbors to their way of thinking. Both of these can lead to fanaticism. I sincerely believe that setting a living example before our neighbors is the most effective ministry we can offer, in the long run. Remember, please, I'm not so much advocating a pluralistic society as I am describing what already exists, and I'm talking not about witnessing to Christ but about trying to get others to adopt our own standards of behavior."

"I was impressed with what Dr. Belgrave said about the teaching of relationships as a major part of the school curriculum. My question is, how can behavior be taught in the classroom?"

"We can do so only to a limited extent. We can explain the principles that lie behind meaningful relationships. Well-adjusted teachers can set an example to the students. But that's about all; and we also know that enlightenment alone won't bring about major behavior changes.

"That's why I think we'll have to create new types of schools. The present classroom is intended primarily for communicating information—conveying systematized knowledge. In a school set up to help build fulfilling relationships, we'd use more dynamic methods—counseling, roleplaying, small group interaction, and other forms of experiencing. We know how to do this with some effectiveness. I believe we really could put on effective programs for young people—in cooperation with their families—that could give them far better training for marriage and parenthood than we have ever provided before."

"Let's take another question."

"This one is for Dr. Stevenson. She said that in the future, relationships based on duty wouldn't work. But isn't a sense of duty necessary to keep all relationships going?"

"Yes. Meaningful relationships involve us in obligations. But I was speaking of relationships devoid of any significant degree of fulfillment and satisfaction. There are marriages that become destructive to the partners; and even the Roman Catholic Church, which does not sanction divorce, doesn't insist that people in that kind of relationship go on living together. Duty is a noble sentiment, but I can see no virtue in having people go on for a lifetime in a relationship that is devoid of all human warmth, that brings no satisfaction. People have been required to continue in such relationships in the past. I don't think this will happen as frequently in the future."

"Another question?"

"One thing I've missed in this discussion is talk about commitment. When you talk about marriage or family or any other relationship, it seems to me that the single key factor which makes any relationship work is commitment. When people are committed to each other, they can work past their difficulties. Not always immediately, but they can if they stay at it. I get really concerned about the marriages that start today and break up in a year and then the divorced people are off to another fling with new people. What about commitment? Wouldn't that change things?"

"Of course it would. And lack of commitment is the reason for many failures."

"Dr. Russell, I'm sorry to interrupt but I'm troubled by some of the words you use. When you throw around words like commitment, I'm never exactly sure what you mean. Can you explain that a little more?"

"I think our present generation probably overtaxes that word commitment. A few minutes ago, someone spoke of duty and I used the word obligation. That's part of the idea of commitment. It involves a deliberate decision. When my son enlisted in the Navy last year he knew he was committing himself to four years of service. Actually, a few years ago we used words like *dedication* to express the same idea. I wonder if that helps any?"

"Yes, thanks. I suppose it's not the word so much but the idea—that it takes a full giving of yourself to make a relationship work."

V

"Exactly! Now we'll break up into our groups. I hope that you'll carry out discussions on some of the issues and questions we've already raised.

"In addition, I'd like you to think about a few others. How would *you* define commitment? Can there be commitment without duty or obligation involved?

"What kind of future do you envision? How will families of the future be similar to those of today? How will they be different?

"What light can Biblical and theological truths throw on the life-style of the Christian family of the future? What should we be aiming at? How do we reach our goal?

"You may want to look back at some of the Biblical material you used in the first session. Some passages that face the issue of permissiveness vs holding to traditional standards are listed."

Matthew 23:25–28
John 8:2–11
Romans 12:1–2; 14:1–15:6
1 John 2:15–17

Chapter 9

New Patterns for Marriage

"THIRTY YEARS AGO, few people would have believed that marriage, an institution at least as old as civilization, would be under serious attack here in the United States. But that is what's happened. At least, our traditional pattern of marriage has been attacked, and proposals have been made to replace it with startling alternatives.

"Tonight we are going to look at these alternatives. I have invited two speakers to share with me in this session. The first is an old friend, Dr. Arthur Jones. This is his second appearance in our course."

I

"Thank you, Pastor Russell. My previous visit to this group was a very pleasant experience.

"As you have said, the critical mood that has developed in our time has mounted attacks on our most honored institutions—including marriage and the family. These attacks are disturbing to many of us. Yet, as a sociologist, I find them challenging, too! In a time of rapid social change, we can't assume that any of our traditional institutions are so sacrosanct that they are above criticism. Marriage as we have known it in the past must justify its existence in the changed conditions of today's world. If it needs modification, let's do something about it. If it really *is* outdated and unworkable, sooner or later we must face the fact.

71

"Let's begin by asking ourselves what we mean by the word 'marriage.' Edward Westermarck, a pioneer in the study of the subject, gave us a definition back in 1891. It's rather involved, but it's worth thinking about. Here it is:

> Marriage is a relation of one or more men to one or more women which is recognized by custom or law and involves certain rights and duties both in the case of the parties entering the union and in the case of the children born of it.

"You will notice at once that this is a very broad definition. It covers all the alternative patterns I'll be describing to you. Therefore we need to remember that what we are talking about here is not a number of life-styles that stand in *opposition* to marriage, but a number of marriage patterns that exist as *alternatives* to the particular form of marriage to which we have been accustomed in our Western culture. The people who advocate these new patterns are not demanding that we give up our traditional form of marriage. They ask only that we also recognize other forms which some members of our culture prefer to adopt. They contend that just as people are free to choose the religion they practice, so they should also be free to choose the marriage form that suits them.

"All I have time to do is describe briefly some of the alternative forms that have been practiced fairly widely in recent years. I'll confine myself to five of them.

"The first is marriage by stages. We find it in two forms. One of these was proposed by Judge Ben Lindsey in his book *The Companionate Marriage*, published in 1927, and was revived in 1966 by Margaret Mead as the 'two step marriage.' The idea is that young people should be allowed to enter into a provisional or trial marriage, during which no children should be born. Later, if this is a success, they move into a more binding commitment in which children might be born and raised. Although this has never been legally recognized, it has been practiced by young people, and by some older people too, in the form of cohabitation followed later by legal marriage. The other form of marriage by stages is a three- or five-year renewable contract, which would enable the couple to break up, without any need for divorce proceedings, whenever the contract runs out.

"The second pattern is serial marriage or sequential marriage. This means simply the right of divorce and remarriage, which Americans have long taken for granted. But many people feel we should be more vocal in approving of a sequence of marriages; this would, they maintain, eliminate the sense of failure or disgrace about changing partners. It would recognize that life-long marriage to the same partner is unworkable for many people.

"The third pattern is marriage which allows both partners sexual freedom. Nena O'Neill and George O'Neill call this 'open marriage' in a book by the same title. Albert Ellis called this 'civilized adultery.' Adultery *is* the legal name for this, of course. The argument runs that adultery has become commonly acknowledged in our culture, so it is more honest to recognize this, as both husbands and wives allow each other the freedom to do openly what was previously done furtively.

"The fourth pattern is plural marriage or polygamy. One form of polygamy—the marriage of one man to several women—has been widely practiced in Africa and elsewhere. The other form—polyandry, or the marriage of one woman to several men—has existed in a few places, such as Tibet and South India. As you know, there have been experimental revivals of plural marriage among young people in our culture in recent years.

"The fifth pattern is group marriage, or multilateral marriage, which goes a step further by including more than one partner of each sex. It can easily be confused with the arrangement in some communes where sexual freedom is practiced by all the members. You can't draw an exact dividing line between the two patterns. But group marriage normally involves only a small number of people who accept a binding commitment both as marriage partners to each other and as parents to all of their children.

"I'll mention one other pattern, which would not come under Westermarck's definition. This is the homosexual marriage, in which two or more persons of the same sex enter into a relationship serious enough to be compared to our concept of marriage. As you know, claims have been made that such marriages should be legally recognized.

"That completes my list of new marriage patterns. But I would like a final word about the way in which we describe them as 'alternatives.' Alternatives to what?

"Those who champion the new patterns often try to justify their arguments by describing what they call 'traditional monogamy' as a dying institution, soon to be replaced by these newer forms. They dwell on the rigidity, the legal and institutional aspects, and the male dominance and female subservience that they say are typical of our traditional marriages. They contend that monogamy is out of place in our new and open society.

"What they fail to acknowledge is that this rigid pattern is already being replaced by what the American family sociologist Ernest W. Burgess described, way back in 1945, as the 'companionship marriage'—a comradeship of equals, free from the rigidities of the past and based on a depth relationship involving openness and the creative sharing of life. This new style of monogamy is the alternative already chosen by millions of American couples, and it differs almost as much from the rigid-styled monogamy of the past as many of the highly publicized new styles. It is my own view that his companionship type of monogamy is the preferred marriage pattern of the majority of people in our culture, and that it has already proven itself to be highly effective and deeply satisfying to those who practice it."

"Dr. Jones, I'm a little tired of the hammering away at what you and others have been calling 'traditional' marriage. You make it sound as though every marriage before 1945 and Ernest Burgess was a rigid, male-dominated, female-exploited marriage.

"I am 69 years old. My husband and I were married *before* 1945. He's always treated me as an equal. We've shared a lot together, and our companionship has been a highlight in our marriage. Frankly, I resent your insistence upon labeling marriages of previous generations with stereotyped concepts."

Several people clap their hands.

"You are quite right to challenge me. Certainly there have been satisfying marriages from the beginning. Every marriage in the past was not dehumanizing. And it *is* unfair to label *all* marriages that way.

"However, I think you will agree that it has been only in quite recent years that we have seen the emergence of a pattern of marriage where husbands and wives are equal in all areas. I don't mean to include every single marriage. I've been speaking in generalities. Perhaps it is more correct to say we are speaking out against unhealthy marriages.

"I want to add that when I say 'unhealthy' I refer to marriages where there is ownership: where one mate owns the other by making him or her dependent. Often the wife is financially and socially dependent upon her husband. Instead of an opportunity for personal growth, there was in effect a denial of personhood. Another feature was rigid role behavior. For instance, I can hardly think of any marriages of the last century where the husband by deliberate choice stayed home with the children and 'kept house' while his wife worked. Modern alternatives would allow this kind of freedom."

"Thank you, Dr. Jones. You've certainly offered us some provocative material.

II

"Now I want to introduce Roger Prentice, a graduate student in psychology. We asked him to present a case for the new life-styles. Roger himself is a member of a multilateral marriage. Welcome to our series, Roger."

"Thank you, Dr. Russell. I'll level with you folks right away, and admit that I came here tonight very much on the defensive. When Dr. Russell told me what you were doing, and invited me to come along, I felt this was a challenge I couldn't miss. But I expected to be violently attacked as a wicked young man without morals, and I came prepared for a fight.

"However, as I listened to Dr. Jones I began to relax. In fact, by the time he finished I felt there wasn't much left for me to say. I realized that I didn't need to plead for tolerance, because I saw that you really are trying to look at all sides of this subject. So I'm not going to give the speech I prepared. Instead I'd like to tell you about how I came to be involved in all this, and maybe then you can ask me some questions.

"To start with my own background, I didn't learn much about healthy marriages at home. My dad was involved in his business and away from home a lot. My mother did her best to raise my sister and me, but she was pretty unhappy, especially when she got to know that Dad was sleeping around with other women. They fought all the time and finally got divorced just as my sister graduated from college and I finished high school. My sister got an overseas job with an oil company. I stayed on with Mother and spent some of my vacations with Dad, who soon remarried. But I wasn't really close to either of them, and I was glad to get away to college.

"My real life revolved around my peer group, both boys and girls. At college I had pretty free relationships for a couple of years, but then I met a great person, Marge, and we decided to live together. We had some rough times, but I remembered how much my dad had hurt my mother by leaving her, and I decided I didn't want to do that to Marge. Marge helped me realize how little I understood about intimate relationships, and I tried to learn to do better. We lived together until college graduation, and then we got married.

"When we moved to graduate school, we lived in a commune near the campus. Most of the others in the commune were fairly free sexually. When they first asked Marge and me to join in, we were against it. We rapped about this with the others over and over. Finally Marge and I, another married couple, and one unmarried girl, decided that we would set up a group marriage among ourselves. We left the commune and rented a house where we have all lived together for the past year.

"That's my story. I'm legally married to Marge, but we lived together unmarried for nearly two years; then about half a year in the commune; and in this group marriage for a year. So I guess I've personally experienced quite a few of Dr. Jones' alternative life-styles.

"I could share with you some impressions of my experiences, but maybe it would be better if I let you ask me questions."

"I'd like to ask if you belong to any church."

"No, none of us do. My folks used to be Methodists. As a kid I went to Sunday school. But religion was just a kind of formal thing in our home—it never had any personal meaning. Marge and I have read some religious books, and we talk about God sometimes. Frankly, religion isn't very important to us. Also, I may be wrong, but I have an idea that the church-going folks would like to run us out of town!"

"Mr. Prentice, do you have any children?"

"Marge is now pregnant. She's also finishing up her master's degree. We tease her that the baby and the sheepskin may arrive together!

"The other couple in our group marriage have two children. All of us help care for them. That's one advantage in multilateral marriage: the kids have alternative parent figures to choose from!"

"Is it in order to ask about sex in a group marriage? I mean, what are the rules?"

"Sure it's okay to ask. But don't get the idea that sex is the central issue, because it isn't. We *live* together. We share the money and divide the work load. Sex is only a small part of it. Really, there are no rules. We don't rotate around the beds, or anything like that. The understanding is that any man and woman can arrange to sleep together, as long as no one objects. Actually, we're more like brothers and sisters in our relationships so the sex part isn't any real problem."

"What about jealousy?"

"Jealousy can be a problem in this kind of marriage. Both Marge and I have had to deal with it. We try to be very open about our feelings, and we talk about them, and work through our problems together. Jealousy is mostly based on possessiveness. That's one thing we want to get out of our systems. None of us *owns* anyone. We're all free human beings. It isn't always easy, though, I admit."

"Would it upset you if Marge turned out to be pregnant by the other man in your group marriage?"

"We're pretty sure that isn't the case. But if we're wrong, it wouldn't bother either of us. We like Jim. Like I said, we're all part of one family."

"What about money and work? How do you share them?"

"Well, it's like a marriage of two people. We try to share the responsibilities. Marge and I agreed to take on most of the cooking and housework, because as students we don't contribute much money. Jim is also a graduate student. But Sally, his legal wife, has a job, and so has Betty. Sally and Betty provide the financial support at present. We don't have much total income right now, so we have to be careful about our spending. We all have a little pocket money for personal needs, but we don't buy any big items unless we're all agreed."

"What happens when you can't reach agreement?"

"The same thing that happens when any loving people disagree. We work toward a compromise. We don't vote, if that's what you mean. I'd like to explain why. If we voted, that would mean majority rule. So if three wanted to go one way and two the other, we'd end up forcing the minority to go along for the sake of harmony. No, we're opposed to that. We're striving toward total freedom and equality. We stay at it until an agreement is reached. Once we talked for nearly eight hours solid, but in the end, we were all happy about the decision."

"Do other group marriages operate like yours?"

"I doubt if any two are alike. People try all kinds of things, and do what seems best to them."

"What do you consider the advantages of a group marriage? What does it offer that monogamy doesn't?"

"Well, I guess Marge and I first joined the commune because we felt it would be good to be closely related to a wider circle of people. This was a way of expressing belief in the idea of being part of a real community. We also felt that it would be good for our own personal growth. Then we found the life of the commune very complicated, and we decided a smaller group, with more commitment to each other, would be better. So we moved into the group marriage.

"Dr. Jones referred to the O'Neills' book *Open Marriage.* I believe we're after the same basic goals they advocate. I will read one paragraph from the speech I had prepared for you and the ideas are based on something I read in that book.

"Group marriage offers the potential for non-dependent living, for personal growth, individual freedom, flexible roles, mutual trust and expansion of ourselves through enrichment."

"Is it your idea to stay in this group marriage all your lives?"

"To be honest with you, I doubt it. We've had a good experience, and I think we've learned a lot. When I finish my Ph.D. in another year or so, we'll probably have to move away. Jim and Sally may do the same. I just don't know about the future."

"Do you feel that you and Marge would be happy alone together again, after this different kind of experience?"

"There are some things we might miss, but I think we'd be okay. As I explained, after the first year or so we've maintained a very good and open relationship with each other."

III

"Excuse me, Roger, for breaking in at this point. You have been very gracious in answering our questions, and you've given us a pretty clear picture of one of the new marriage patterns. Now I'd like to look at these new developments in our culture in the light of our Christian faith.

"Modern Christians are learning to live in a democracy, where we don't try to coerce others, and others don't coerce us. It's a matter of peaceful coexistence—like an open market where merchants spread out their wares and the buyers go for what look like the best buys. To put it another way, we still believe our way of life to be the best, but we're learning to accept the competition of those who think otherwise.

"Roger, you represent the competition. To some extent you

make us feel uncomfortable. I wouldn't be surprised to hear that some of our church members take the view that I shouldn't have invited you to speak in our course. Outside the church, we hear about our competitors all the time. I think it's good once in a while for us to invite them in to talk with us..

"In this course we have already seen that some concepts of marriage and the family must change. They must be adapted to new conditions in a new world. As a matter of fact, not a few of our ideas of Christian family life have already changed. For instance, we tolerate divorce, even if we don't approve; we accept birth control; male dominance is passing away; authoritarian attitudes to child rearing simply aren't functional in our freer world. But as we accept these changes, we find ourselves wondering how far we can allow ourselves to go. How much more must we change?

"It's natural to fear change—especially as we grow older. But I'm encouraged to believe we're open to change, even if a little fearful. Most of us know that as responsible Christians we can't separate ourselves from the modern world. Our task is to make our message relevant to the era in which we are living.

"Some of the things Roger has talked about are of great interest and concern to us—achieving harmonious relationships between men and women; developing a sense of community; growing into greater maturity; providing the best possible setting for raising our children. Perhaps some of the people who are offering alternatives to traditional marriage are just trying to tear down the Establishment, with nothing very promising to put in its place. We are justifiably afraid of such people. But I don't see Roger Prentice, as he has presented himself here, as that kind of person. I see him as an idealist. After his experience of his parents' unhappy marriage, I understand his lack of confidence in what he calls the conventional pattern, and in these circumstances it was natural that he should be prepared to try something new and different.

"I was encouraged by what Dr. Jones said at the end of his presentation about the new kind of companionship marriage that is already taking the place of the traditional form. And it's encouraging that Roger and Marge still see their relationship to each other as being central. Maybe what's wrong with us Christians is that we have failed to present convincing examples of fulfillment in marriage, so that the world hasn't seen enough of what a truly Christian marriage is like. Maybe in the competitive marketplace our goods have looked a little shoddy, and because of that it isn't surprising that many of our young people have decided that they might do better with new patterns.

IV

"Our failure—or whether there's been a failure—is one of the more important things you may want to talk about together.

"Some other subjects that come immediately to mind are: Do we feel that the traditional marriage has a future? Do you think that the companionship type of relationship, representing equality, depth-relationship, and the creative sharing of life, can be achieved in the alternatives we've mentioned? What about some of the alternatives Dr. Jones described: marriage by stages, serial marriage, marriage with sexual freedom, group marriage, homosexual marriage?

"Then, how do you react to the experiences of Roger Prentice? What can we learn, if anything, from him and his group? How far can and should Christian standards be modified to meet the changing conditions of our new world?

"Again tonight we have no special Biblical material before us, but some of the basic passages on the family and on human relationships are listed here, and they could help strengthen your discussion.

"Thank you, Dr. Jones and Mr. Prentice, for your stimulating presentations. Now let's go to our groups."

Genesis 2: 18–25
Matthew 19:3–9
Romans 12:9–21
1 Corinthians 12:14–13:3
Galatians 5:13–26

Chapter 10

New Patterns for Parenthood

"THIS EVENING WE'RE going to look at some of the most disturbing possibilities that have ever arisen to challenge women and men. Scientific probing has at last brought us to the point at which we may soon have power to manipulate human life at its very source. The result of this new knowledge could lead to the most frightening events in the whole of human history.

"I wanted to make this statement at the very beginning of our tenth session to prepare us to face very controversial issues. As we look at new patterns for parenthood, we'll begin with what is called the new biology. However, that's only one part of our subject. The other part deals with new ideas about raising children once they are born.

"I have invited two special speakers to join me for this session. The first is Dr. Ellen Parker, an obstetrician-gynecologist who practices in our city. Dr. Parker, welcome to our program."

I

"Thank you, Pastor. I hope I can do justice to the assignment you have given me. Reproductive biology and genetics are very complicated subjects. To condense their findings into nontechnical language in a brief space of time isn't going to be easy. However, I've agreed to try, so here we go!

"For the people of Bible times, reproduction was both a miracle and a mystery. But with the invention of the microscope in the seventeenth century, the mystery began to be unveiled. First came the discovery of sperm and ovum. Then, in our present century, we discovered chromosomes and genes. From these key discoveries, we have gone on to unlock the secrets of life itself. And with knowledge has come power—power to do what has never been done before.

"The first major use of the power came with the development of contraception, which enabled us to separate sexual intercourse and reproduction, and thus to control the number of children a couple produced. Then we enabled childless couples to have children. The most controversial means of doing this was artificial insemination, which made it possible to make a woman pregnant without intercourse by injecting sperm from her husband, or from an anonymous donor if the husband was sterile. This created a furor at first and complicated legal problems are still pending in our courts. But it is estimated there are now 150,000 people conceived by artificial insemination in the United States alone.

"The next problem tackled was to enable parents to choose the sex of their children in advance. This was first attempted with animals, and then applied to humans. A high degree of success has been claimed for the procedures that are used.

"Next, scientists tackled the problem of what is called the 'test-tube baby.' The first experiments attempted to bring about conception—the union of sperm and ovum—outside the woman's body. Attempts to do this were begun at Harvard Medical School in 1944, and success was demonstrated in 1952 at Columbia University. A human egg, fertilized by sperm in a laboratory dish, grew to the point at which it was ready to be implanted in the womb of a future mother. There was some hesitation about actually doing this, because the subject was so controversial. But the transplanting of a fertilized ovum was successfully carried out in England in 1974. It is now possible for one woman to 'give' her beginning baby to another.

"Based on those successful experiments, it is probably only a matter of time until an egg cell taken from a woman's body and fertilized by a sperm cell taken from a man's body will grow into a human baby in an artificial womb. This would make parenthood possible without sexual intercourse, without pregnancy, and without childbirth. Or a woman could receive a fertilized egg from a donor man and woman who have been carefully selected so that the future child's makeup can be determined in advance—its sex,

IQ, eye color, hair color, and any other special qualities that are desired.

"This gets us into genetic engineering. There are some very unpleasant inherited diseases and defects that result in severely handicapped or abnormal children. We now know the genes that are responsible for these conditions. We are also able to tell, early in the woman's pregnancy, if she is carrying a defective child. If she is, the woman could then have an abortion if she wished.

"But we can expect to do more than this. Genetic engineering will be able simply to eliminate the undesirable genes and assure parents that their children will be free from inherited disease. As we have seen, this also means that other characteristics of children can be decided in advance. We could produce as many geniuses as we want."

"Dr. Parker, I think you're presenting your case as though genes work in only one way. Medical research has done a lot to correct genetic defects, but that's a touchy area. Recently I watched a TV program about sickle-cell anemia, which I understand is a genetic abnormality caused by the change of just one amino acid in the molecules of hemoglobin. When the abnormal gene is present in what I think they call 'single copy' it causes a mild respiratory deficiency; in two copies it produces a deadly illness. Somewhere in the future I realize that a drug will be found to destroy this dangerous gene. *But*, and here's where I'm concerned, there are good effects of this sickle-cell gene because, in a single copy, it protects against malaria. Now if that's true with this one gene, how about others? I'm simply saying that I think it's a highly dangerous thing to play around with."

"Thank you. You're quite right. But danger or potential danger is never sufficient reason to stop progress. I'll simply say at this point that the best we can do is work at one defect, one problem, one gene at a time. As our knowledge expands, we move farther along.

"I've only been trying to speak to you in a nontechnical way of the promise we find in genetic engineering. There's still a long road to travel. But remember, when Jules Verne wrote a novel about the submarine everyone laughed and said it could never be. Or how many of us as children saw the weekly movie serials of Flash Gordon fighting in outer space? Who would have believed the possibility of outer space travel? But today, who would doubt it?

"Perhaps the most controversial issue in current genetic research is 'cloning.' The word itself comes from the Greek root meaning 'cutting.' Cloning is generally defined as 'asexual propagation.' This means simply reproduction without sex. Cloning makes it possible for a woman to bear a child without the necessary union of egg and sperm. More incredibly, it also makes possible the birth of a child whose *only* parent is a male. In either case, the cloned offspring will have only one parent and will become the *identical* twin of that parent.

"Cloning has already been done successfully in frogs. If it were feasible in humans it could be used to produce many copies of the same individual, many identical twins, or rather multiplets. What would be the status of these clonal twins? Would they suffer from *not* being unique? Or, conversely, would they draw from their biological identity with multiple siblings a new sense of human communion?

"Frankly, it's impossible to foresee the consequences of potential new biotechnologies because there is no way to evaluate the interactions with the social settings in which they may become available and be applied. In a competitive, caste-ridden, power-dominated society, the ability to refashion human beings either by selection or by manipulations of eggs, sperm, and genes might become a tool to promote inequality and oppression. It might serve to create masses of obediently toiling slaves or to manufacture elites of identical rulers. The greater our powers, the greater the risks. But, the opportunities are great, too. I, for one, don't feel that we should hold back in any area of potential progress even though we need to be alerted to the dangers."

"Dr. Parker, we realize the difficult task we gave you and we want to say thank you. I hope this will provoke further discussions in the small groups.

II

"In the meantime, however, let's take a look at another aspect of parenthood—what we do with children after they're born, or hatched, or delivered, or whatever the correct term is. To deal with this subject, we invited Dr. Evelyn Whittier, a specialist in the field of child development, to come and speak to us. You will remember that in our third session Jim Darnell reported at length on an interview with her. Dr. Whittier, what we learned from you then was most helpful. Tonight we're delighted you can be here yourself."

"Thank you, Pastor. There was a time when discussions of parenthood had to begin with the child's birth, because we knew so little about what went before. Now our knowledge is stretching in all directions. That's a good thing, because knowledge is power—although power must be used responsibly and with discretion.

"When I talked to Jim, I stressed the fact that nothing provides a better setting for healthy emotional and social development of the child than to be raised by two loving parents who have a good relationship to each other. I firmly believe that.

"I also pointed out, however, that parenting in today's complicated world is a very difficult task for which not all parents are qualified. The inevitable consequence is that we are producing many emotionally disturbed and socially maladjusted people. Of course such people in turn are poorly qualified to be good parents themselves. All this is happening at a time when our understanding of child development has reached higher levels than ever before.

"This combination of circumstances is leading some people to believe that, in the interests of our cultural future, we must initiate radical changes. Let me outline what is now being proposed.

"Since parenthood shapes our future citizens, and since many fathers and mothers are unqualified either through lack of training or ability or both, why not turn the job over to professionals? Why not select married couples who have the right qualities, thoroughly train them, pay them well, and set them to work as professional child-raisers? Many parents find their task pretty discouraging, and they feel guilty about the ineffective job they are doing. All right, let's encourage them to hand over their children to experts, while maintaining their basic relationship by having the children visit them regularly and taking them off on special trips and vacations.

"Would parents do this? Actually they *have* done it in some countries. For generations, upper class English parents have turned their children over to Nannies and then sent them off to boarding schools from as early as seven years of age. Or, more radically, some Russian parents, in a classless society, relinquish their responsibilities in child rearing. Parents in the Israeli kibbutzim hand over their children's upbringing to people specially assigned for the job.

"If parents won't agree to do this, some think that eventually the government will intervene. Already law courts can take away children from negligent or unfit parents. It might be necessary to establish tests for parental competence, possibly even requiring parents to hold a certificate showing satisfactory training in order to keep their children.

"Another solution favored in some quarters is to set up large, family-like groupings, like the extended families in some other cultures. This arrangement would provide children with many parent figures. This would lessen the possibility of a child's suffering emotional damage from too close a supervision by an incompetent, hostile, or emotionally disturbed mother or father.

"All these proposed new patterns have the same aim. They declare that we cannot afford to go on allowing children to suffer emotional maladjustment by being deprived of warm, loving, and skilled parenting. Deprivation is a cruel injustice to the children concerned, a tragic waste of human resources, and a burden to our culture.

"Well, that's the problem, and these are some of the new solutions being proposed. This part of parenthood is just as controversial as the other. What we want and need is a generation of children who are well born and well raised. Then we'll have the resources we need to build a better world."

"Dr. Whittier, I'm Nora Robinson and I can't sit still any longer. You pushed for turning the raising of our children over to the professionals. But one thing disturbs me. I'm a Christian. I sincerely believe that Jesus Christ is Savior and Lord. I also believe that God entrusts to my care the responsibility for my children and holds me responsible for them. That includes their religious training. You're suggesting that professionals do the training. I suppose that means religious instructions, too? Like professional Baptists, professional Lutherans? [laughter] I'm not trying to make a joke out of this! I'm not sure that I could let that happen. One reason for having children is to share with them the experiences of daily living, of influencing them with the values and attitudes you hold. I'm not a perfect parent, but I love my children. And it seems to me that loving children and caring for them is the best thing any child-raiser can do.

"I suppose what I'm reacting to most strongly is your implication that 98% of all parents are failures. Frankly, I resent that kind of insinuation, Dr. Whittier!"

"I really stepped into that one! I'm going to let most of what you say go unanswered, not because I agree, but I think you'll get more out of discussing this question in your groups. I only want to add that I *don't* feel 98% of parents are failures. I do feel there *is* greater failure—or at least a greater sense of failure and frustration—among parents now than at any other time. And it's such a shame because we understand so much more about human behavior."

"Dr. Whittier, I agree, and I think Mrs. Robinson won't mind saving that for her group, will you?"

She nods yes.

"Dr. Whittier, we're grateful for your presentation.

III

"I believe all of us listened to our speakers with some feelings of apprehension. We honor and respect our scientists; but when they probe with their instruments into those sensitive areas where the mystery of life itself is enshrined, we almost feel that they are desecrating holy places, and should be stopped."

Pastor Russell continues. "As I examine my reactions, however, I wonder whether I am prejudiced. We believe this is God's world. Someone once said that science is thinking God's thoughts after him. As our understanding of ourselves becomes broader and deeper, we can repeat with the psalmist that we are fearfully and wonderfully made. As our minds are stretched in their attempt to grasp the staggering immensity of the universe, and the amazing intricacy of human cells, too small to be seen without a microscope, we find the same all-pervading beauty and order that confront us in a spider's web or a wayside flower. We are reminded of the creation story, when God looked at all that he had made and saw that it was very good.

"Another thought that comes to me is that these new discoveries are not just a matter of idle curiosity. They offer the possibility of preventing and overcoming crippling diseases. Anything that offers us the chance to make human life better ought to be welcomed. There are dangers involved, but that's true of every action we perform. Anything good in the world can be misused and exploited by people for evil purposes. All new benefits that come to us involve us in new risks.

"It seems therefore that we can only move into an uncertain future with the faith and hope that in the end we'll gain more than we lose because of this new knowledge. We don't really have a choice. The human mind is not going to be turned aside from its quest for better understanding of the world.

"So we struggle with our new knowledge and power, and try to see how they can be put to the best use. As we have stressed before during this series, we Christians have no right to make negative judgments against our culture if we stand aside and take no part in the critical decisions being made. In a democratic society we have as much right to be heard as anyone else has. But we won't be listened to if we don't know what's going on and join in the struggle to come up with workable solutions. And who will believe our solutions are workable if we can't demonstrate that we have made them work for ourselves?

IV

"Let's stop now so you can ask questions. Who'll be the first?"

"Dr. Parker, why would women want to have their babies made for them by a machine? Don't you think it's important to a woman to nurture her child in her own body, and bring it into the world when it is ready to be born?"

"Many women feel like that. But we also know that women have changed remarkably in recent years. Some people thought the mothering instinct would cause women to feel revulsion against the idea of abortion, but for large numbers of women that hasn't happened. Don't we welcome a machine that will save us effort and inconvenience? Being pregnant, I can assure you, involves a woman in a great deal of inconvenience. And childbirth can be very painful. I can't venture to guess how many other women would be willing to hand all this over to a machine, but I would."

"Dr. Whittier, can you *really* train people to be good parents? Aren't some people just naturally endowed with the necessary qualities, while others aren't?"

"To some extent that's true. There are also people who are great with babies and hopeless with teenagers! Parenthood is a very complex task requiring not only certain qualities, but great versatility in using those qualities. I also believe that most of us have the broad combination of capacities needed. The shortcomings of parents are usually due to the fact that they don't really understand how children function, and what can and can't be expected of them. Lacking that understanding, they make mistakes and alienate their children. Then the children react with hostility, and the parents find their efforts so frustrating and unrewarding that they give up trying. Well trained parents, supported by skilled supervisors, wouldn't get into this kind of mess. The critical issue in parenting is to be able to enjoy it and find it rewarding when parent and child healthily *enjoy* their interaction, the results are almost always good."

"Dr. Whittier, your assumption is based on a kind of naive faith in behavioral science. I'm more skeptical; I don't think you're being realistic. I am a teacher with eight years' experience. I know how hard it is to love all the children in my classes equally. Some children are very hard to do anything with, no matter what I try. Even with my experience and my training, I haven't made it come out right as either a teacher or a parent. I don't look upon myself as a failure, only that I'm human. I've achieved some success. But when you make such general statements about the problems and then make your solutions sound so easy, I have trouble staying with you."

"You have the right to disagree with me, sir. I'm trying to be honest. I sincerely believe in what I've presented here tonight. Perhaps I've been guilty of oversimplification or overgeneralization, but I also have to say that I've seen excellent results, too!"

"Dr. Whittier, it sounds to me as if most of the new patterns for parenthood want to take the child out of the home into some kind of institution. I always thought institutional child care didn't work well."

"That has certainly been true of many institutions—orphanages, for example. But we mustn't make harsh judgments, because orphanages have often had to deal with very disturbed and deprived children. Also, our best childcare institutions have learned to reproduce the family model as far as possible—households, with the children living with married couples. There has been a lot of controversy about the Israeli kibbutzim and the Russian boarding schools. Experts are divided about the effectiveness of their methods. However, most of the reformers favor putting children in normal family settings, but with highly qualified foster-parents. The only thing lacking would be a blood relationship, and nowadays we don't consider that to be as important as it was thought to be in the past."

"Dr. Parker, I'd like to ask about genetic engineering. Apart from avoiding inherited diseases, what advantages would this have?"

"Oh, quite a few. It has already worked wonders with plants and animals. For example, Dr. F. C. Steward of Cornell University took cells from a carrot root and within three weeks had multiplied the carrot eighty times! Similar experiments have been perfected with tobacco plants. Now scientists are working with grains and other edible products. We have bred animals for special purposes. At the human level, it would be possible to give people bodies that served them better. For example, if we could make brain cells that would renew themselves as body cells do, old age could be much less distressing. If we could give people hearts with larger coronary arteries, our greatest killer disease would lose much of its destructive power."

V

"Thank you, Drs. Parker and Whittier, for a very informative, challenging, provocative session. Now let's go to our groups and continue the discussion.

"For Biblical background on parenthood, we can go back to passages we had before us in the third session. In addition, as we think of the new developments Dr. Parker has described, we might want to contrast the pessimism of Ecclesiastes 1 with the hope for the future in Isaiah 65:17–25, or the despair of people in a new, bad situation reflected in Psalm 137 with the trust in God's greatness seen in Psalm 139."

Chapter 11
New Patterns for Communal Living

I

"AT THE BEGINNING of our Bible, in Genesis 2, we read that God, having made a man in his own image, decided that it was not good for him to be alone. He created a woman to keep him company and to be his helper. God gave the man and the woman the sexual ability to create new beings, to fulfill the divine command, 'Be fruitful and multiply.'

"Thus from the beginning of human history we see that relationships are part of the essential nature of human life. Hermits have chosen to live alone, and sometimes shipwrecked sailors have had no alternative, but in general human beings are incurably social. They need one another, and without interpersonal relationships life would be pretty meaningless for almost all of us.

"The most basic human communities have been families. As was pointed out earlier in this series, family life has always been the central form of community life for the Jews. However, it has not been the *only* form of community, for the Jews or anyone else.

"Actually, the idea of communal living about which we hear so much today is not new. It's been found in almost all periods of world history. Thus at the time of Jesus, a zealous, ascetic Jewish community called the Essenes lived near the Dead Sea. They were the ones who wrote and then hid the famous Dead Sea Scrolls, discovered only a few years ago. Some scholars believe that John the Baptist was at one time a member of this community.

"The history of the infant Christian church in the Acts of the Apostles tells about believers setting up what today would be called a commune. It's worth rereading the highlights of that story as found in Acts 4:32, 34–35:

> Now the company of those who believed were of one heart and one soul, and no one said that any of the things which he possessed was his own, but they had everything in common. . . . There was not a needy person among them, for as many as were possessors of lands or houses sold them, and brought the proceeds of what was sold and laid it at the apostles' feet; and distribution was made to each as any had need.

We don't know the final details of that story. Probably, because of the great persecution described later in Acts, the Jerusalem church's leaders were scattered so widely that the communal idea was abandoned. That the community had financial problems is clear from Paul's taking up a collection for them, and this too may have been due to persecution, which would make it hard for believers to get jobs in Jerusalem.

"In the Christian church after the apostolic age, a different kind of communal living emerged. Scholars date 270 as the beginning of monasticism. Originally such hermits were not organized into an actual community, but each practiced the ascetic life in closely adjoining caves. Communal monasticism made its appearance about fifty years later.

"Originally begun as lay movements, these groups put their emphasis on a search for holiness, for closeness to God. In time, this led to celibacy, and the participants eventually became the 'holy orders' of the medieval church. Monks and nuns were required to take the threefold vow of poverty, chastity, and obedience. The Roman Catholic Church has maintained its monastic communities, and they are still based on the renunciation of property, of sex and marriage, and of the final right to make individual decisions about one's own life.

"Since the Reformation, a number of other religious communities have been established, such as the Bruderhof in 1528, the Shakers in 1774, and the Oneida Community in 1842. Unlike the Catholic communities, they generally included both men and women. In some, conventional marriage was allowed; in others it was not. The Shakers, for instance, practiced strict celibacy. They defended their stance in a pamphlet, first printed in 1868, in which they said they did not condemn marriage entirely, nor consider procreation wrong. But they felt that 'the great Architect has divers grades of workmen, all necessary in their places ... to complete the building.' Even in nature, the Shakers asserted, millions of seeds never germinate. Before you ask, I'll mention that they increased their membership by recruitment of adults and adoption of orphans.

"Nowadays, when many experiments in group living are taking place, we remind ourselves that the local church is in itself a kind of communal center in which people share worship, fellowship, and service to others, and through which we also share part of our worldly goods. It must be admitted that the record of the more intensive Christian experiments in communal living, apart from the rigidly disciplined Roman Catholic ones, has shown that they tend not to last for long. It seems that there are some pretty formidable difficulties in maintaining such systems on a voluntary basis. But we Christians are always ready to admire idealists, because we are idealists ourselves. So I hope we'll be sympathetic toward experiments going on around us today.

"Our guest speakers will talk about these contemporary experiments, with special emphasis on the extent to which they try to be alternatives to the family. Our first speaker is Dr. Norman Edwards, Associate Professor of Sociology at Fieldstone College. He will give us a broad account of what communes are all about."

II

"Thanks, Dr. Russell. I have never lived in a commune myself, but I have visited several and talked to their members, in addition to doing extensive reading about the movement. This is a brief summary of my conclusions.

"Human beings in relation to other humans seem to have three kinds of needs. First, they need a community of intimacy, where they can be understood, loved, and trusted; where they can be themselves without defense or pretense; and where they can gain a sense of their own identity and worth. This has normally been met more or less adequately by belonging to a family or kinship group.

"The other two needs are at opposite extremes from each other. On one side is the need for privacy, to get away and be alone. On the other side is the need to belong to a wider group—a community beyond the family in which you can find friends, choose a marriage partner, learn about the wide world and its ways, and share with others in mutual defense, in exchanges of services, in cultural experiences, in education, in recreation, and so on.

"During long periods of human history, this third need was met by the tribe or clan, which was usually a village made up of a number of separate households.

"As populations increased and big cities appeared, problems arose. On the one hand, it was hard to find privacy. Many people suffered by losing touch with their own inner thoughts and feelings. But the biggest problem was the loss of the tribal or neighborhood group. In the large city, the mutual aid and support of neighbor for neighbor often withered away.

"As cities in America grew, and each person made more and more social contacts, relationships became more impersonal. Attempts were made to find substitutes for the tribal group. Churches helped, and other kinds of clubs and organizations such as the YMCA and YWCA played their part. But as families became more and more mobile, these substitutes failed to meet the needs of many.

"One result was that heavy demands were made on the family to meet a much wider set of emotional and social needs than ever before—while at the same time the mood of our nation was emphasizing individual rights and in consequence putting heavy strains on family relationships. Some families responded by becoming closed-in social groups that tried to meet all the needs of their members and ignored their neighbors. Other families broke down under the strain.

"As I see it, the commune movement is a spontaneous effort on the part of people who feel deprived and want their social needs met. Some are married couples, with or without children, who feel the need of wider and deeper relationships beyond their tight, closed-in circle. Others are men or women who have broken with their families as a result of frustration and disillusionment and who are looking for something to take the family's place. Most of them bring, along with their unmet needs, some degree of idealism. They are rebels against a society which, to them, has become impersonal, materialistic, and hypocritical. Many, perhaps naively, hope that, in addition to meeting their own needs, they may become pioneers of a new social order. Mixed in among the two broad groups I have described is a sprinkling of emotionally disturbed people, and a few who join out of curiosity. Naturally, this isn't unique to communes.

94

"So you can see that it's difficult to generalize about communes today. We have no idea how many have been set up in recent years. Historians estimate that 150 existed in the last century. Recent estimates run as high as 3,000 communes in the United States, with more than 100,000 people participating, most of them ranging in age from late teens to the late 20s, but with a good sprinkling of middle and older adults.

"Speaking broadly, the communal way obviously presents its own problems. The majority of communes don't last more than a few months. Disenchanged communitarians relate tales of jealousy, greed, and general bad feelings; in some cases ordinary family life sounds tranquil and satisfying by comparison. Even in stable communities members have to spend an incredible amount of time and energy simply trying to get along with one another, and this saps them of energy to confront other difficulties of life."

"Dr. Edwards, I'm Jenny Andrews. I've heard about communes for a long time but I've always been confused about what they actually are. Could you give me a brief definition?"

"That's as hard as describing communes. One writer called it, 'any arrangement of three or more persons whose primary bond is some form of common sharing, rather than blood or legal ties.' A half dozen people in a large apartment or house, sharing the rent and splitting the cooking and cleaning duties, might call themselves a commune. Or they might merely call themselves roommates!

"But I will say this. Most of the people with whom I have talked and who live in communes believe that they are involved in some sort of movement, but it is a movement that has no organization, no leadership, and few clearly shared goals. When I say that, I'm talking about the commune movement as a whole, and not about specific communes or groups of communes.

"I hope that gives you an answer to your question.

"I'd like to say a few more things about communal living and the people who join. We do know from research that they are not very constant in their attachment. Many move from one group to another. Others, either satisfied with their experience or disenchanted, go back to the more traditional patterns of living.

"The instability of communes has been criticized as a weakness. But this may not be quite accurate. Most of these people are young, and are in the process of finding themselves. Many of them *do* find answers to their needs through the communal experience, but recognize that they have no wish to continue that experience.

If we consider communal living as a way of spending some of the time that elapses between leaving the parental home and establishing a new conjugal home, it really offers more than life in a rooming house or college dormitory. It's an in-depth experience of sharing with others while learning useful, if sometimes painful, things about oneself.

"Communes that achieve a degree of stability tend to have certain characteristics in common. Perhaps the first one is strong, charismatic leadership. Another is a common sense of purpose—a shared ideology which binds the group together. These two generally lead to a third, an efficient organization. A fourth is frequent opportunities for the members to meet and work through their differences in honest confrontation and give and take. Many of these sessions use encounter group techniques.

"Now I'll say something about communes as substitutes for the family. I'll leave out what we call multilateral or group marriages, which have already been discussed here. They aren't really communes, but only extensions of monogamous marriage to include several husbands and wives instead of just two people.

"Many communes claim to be extended families. They usually consist of married persons, or family groups, who unite to create a larger community of people. They live together and share money and work, but not usually sexual interaction except between members who are legally married to each other. Single persons may join, but essentially this is a family of families, together because they believe life will be better for all in the larger community. Such communes are often set up by religious groups.

"They differ greatly from the traditional extended families of older cultures, which were rigid, hierarchical structures that made some members powerfully dominant and forced the others into submission. Those older ones were held together by a tight discipline far removed from any concept of democracy. Of course, there are still a few communes like that, such as the Children of God—but most are dedicated to democratic principles.

"A variant pattern is the so-called 'family cluster,' in which a group of families join together for mutual support, but stay in their separate homes and try to create the equivalent of an old-fashioned village community or neighborhood group.

"Another type of commune replaces the family with something quite different. These communities practice group sex, as well as sharing work and money. In some, drugs are extensively used.

They tend to be more unstable, because they are made up mainly of individuals and discourage special relationships within the group. New members join as others leave, and sometimes the group breaks up completely. But they claim some benefits. Sexual variety is an obvious one. Also wide opportunities for companionship tend to be valued.

"There's always a tendency, though, to get tired of all the complications and go back to the pair-bond as the most satisfying and least demanding kind of intimate relationship. After a period of group sex, some of these people end up with quite conventional marriages. Some draw an analogy to what happened at times in an older generation, when young men 'sowed their wild oats' and then settled down to establish families. This is only one kind of commune, but it has tended to give them all a bad name among many people.

"To sum up, a lot of learning about human relationships goes on in communes. Life is demanding, but if offers possibilities for a lot of dynamic and creative experiences. In my opinion, however, if families in our culture could cultivate a similar kind of honest communication and openness among their members, a similar respect for the individual's right to experiment and grow, a similar kind of outreach to other people outside the family group, and a similar concern for deeper recognition of human values in our culture generally, most of the communes would have little to offer that people couldn't get at home."

"Thanks, Dr. Edwards."

III

"And now let me introduce Sally Cartwright, who lives in a commune. Welcome, Sally."

"Thank you, Dr. Russell. I think I'll begin with my personal story. First of all, you'll be interested to know that my father is a pastor, like you.

"My parents were very good to me, and taught me about Jesus Christ. But in my late teens I began to feel that many church people didn't really take Jesus seriously. They sang hymns and listened to sermons, but outside the church they seemed mainly concerned with making money and climbing the social ladder. They seemed not to be aware of all the cruel injustices in the world. They enjoyed rich food while poor people starved.

They supported war almost enthusiastically, which to me is a complete denial of all that Jesus taught. They seemed indifferent to the misfortunes of minority groups—blacks, Puerto Ricans, Indians. When I tried to challenge them about such things, they would shake their heads and smile as if I were a very ignorant idealist who merely needed time to grow up to become worldly wise.

"I began to read books about the lives of great Christians, especially missionaries and reformers. I was fascinated by the story of Francis of Assisi, who was born into a wealthy home and surrounded by luxuries. He became more and more uneasy about the way he was living, and finally left it all behind for a life of poverty and simplicity with other men and women who shared his ideals. I felt sure that if I had been alive in his time I would have wanted to join him. I longed to share in a real Christian community like the one he established.

"I know now that a lot of this was starry-eyed idealism. My parents urged me to be content to join in the church life and social life around me. I tried, but it all seemed empty.

"I went to college, and for a time I felt better. I met other young people who were idealistic, and I joined in their activities. I became involved in social action on behalf of minority groups, and in women's liberation. Still I wasn't satisfied. To me Christianity was a total way of life, not just a spare-time hobby.

"One day I heard about a group of people who had taken over a farm and lived together as Christian brothers and sisters. I went to visit them, and was deeply impressed. At the end of my second year in college, I arranged to spend the summer vacation there. That settled it for me. I never went back to college. That was two and a half years ago. I've lived in the commune ever since.

"Not all people join a commune out of commitment to Jesus Christ as I did, but I believe there are some ideals, goals, and dislikes that most communitarians share. One is a profound dissatisfaction with what the middle class calls the American Way of Life—the idea of getting ahead, no matter what the cost, of making money, of acquiring more objects and more status. Many of the older communalists gave up high-paying jobs and expensive homes to get out of the rat race. Younger members often go from college campus to commune, entirely bypassing the rat race. And a lot of parents get uptight about it.

"Dissatisfaction is one reason for joining the commune; a second is the desire to groove with nature. That sounds odd to some of you, perhaps, but the commune movement and ecological awareness are closely connected. Most of the communes I know try to engage in organic gardening; the members prepare natural foods, and many become vegetarians. They place a lot of stress on physical labor as opposed to intellectual. For our commune, getting back to God includes getting back to nature.

"There's a third reason—and, Dr. Edwards, perhaps this one is part of what you've been saying. A common desire is to find new and more satisfying forms of interpersonal relationships. For instance, many feel that the small nuclear family is not a viable institution. They stress that in the past people lived in large family groupings. Grandparents, uncles, aunts, and cousins—all depended upon each other, supported each other. Child rearing was carried on by the entire extended family rather than by parents alone. Today, most people live in a family unit of a mother, a father, and children, with only occasional visits from other relatives. This is not enough. In the commune, we hope to establish the security of the extended family.

"So you can see I'm a staunch defender of communes, at least some of them. I came here tonight partly because I've heard so much about communes put down, as though they're all hotbeds of promiscuous sex and drug abuse. Sure, those things are widespread but certainly no more so—and I believe a lot less—than in the general population. And we don't have any of that in our community. You see, for those of us who have found what we're looking for, raw sex and acid trips aren't for us.

"I could tell you more about how we live together. But maybe it would be better if you asked me questions."

"Sally, how do your parents feel about what you have done?"

"Their feelings are mixed. They were disappointed that I quit college. For a while they were worried about me, because they thought I had gotten myself mixed up with a bunch of crackpots. But last year they visited the farm and stayed a few days. They liked what they saw, and they now seem to accept the fact that this is the life I have chosen. I believe they still think of me as a dreamer, and I'm sure they wonder if I won't leave the community some day."

"Tell us about life in the commune. Describe a typical day."

"Well, we get up early, because most of our work is done on the land. After breakfast we have worship. The work of the day is divided up: inside jobs, outside jobs, visits to town for shopping, and so on. In the evenings we do various things, such as Bible study, group discussions of social issues, classes with visiting teachers, crafts and handwork, and some social activities. Then evening prayers and bed."

"How do you organize yourselves? Do you have a leader? Are some of you married? How do you manage your money?"

"Wait a minute! That's a lot of questions. Yes, we have a leader. Bud Thompson was once the manager of a grocery store, and he's a great organizer. He's 56. His wife, Flo, and their son, Bill, are members of the commune. We have 27 members altogether, and that includes six married couples, nine children, and six unattached singles.

"What else did you ask? How are we organized? We have a meeting of the whole group once a week, usually on Wednesday evenings, when we discuss all our plans for the coming week, share out the duties, and listen to any concerns and complaints. If we have some big decision to make, we may have a special meeting. Bud hears everyone as long as any of us want to talk. Then, he makes the major decisions. But if we disagree with what he decides, we can vote it down. Generally, we trust his wisdom. Oh, and we always pray before we start discussing every subject. We try to follow the teachings of Jesus, as far as we can. We want his will in everything.

"You asked about money. We don't have much, but we don't need much. Our life is simple. Whatever we produce on the land and don't need ourselves, we sell. We also sell things we make in our workshop. There are a number of Christians out in the world who believe in us, and they contribute to our budget."

"Do you go out preaching? I mean, are you evangelists?"

"Yes, sort of. We believe in our way of life. And when you're grooved onto something, you can't shut up—you have to talk about it. Right? But if you mean, like going to people's houses, preaching in parks and on street corners, then the answer is no. We talk to people. Most people, when they get to know me, eventually ask where I live or something like that. Then I tell them what I believe.

"But our group also witnesses by the life we live. We're interracial, and we've rejected sex-role stereotypes—men can cook and women can plow. We've made friends in our rural community. If we hear of neighbors in trouble, we try to help. We visit the sick, and make calls on lonely old people. Visitors occasionally come to see our commune. It blows their minds to realize we're not acid heads or hippies or sex perverts."

"You say you have six 'unattached singles.' Are you one of them?"

"Yes, but I plan to marry next month. John is a Quaker who visited us and shares our ideals. He's a social worker, but is giving up his job and joining our commune."

"Sally, are you satisfied with your life in the commune? Would you consider staying there all your life?"

"I'm happy where I am. Right now I can't think of any other way of life that I'd be happy with."

"Thanks, Sally, and thanks to all of you who have shared with us this evening.

IV

"Before you break up into your groups, I hope you'll think through the questions that have already been asked. Perhaps you'd like to explore them a little more.

"Since the early Christians obviously practiced a form of communal living, why shouldn't we? Is the style of life advocated in the New Testament supposed to be the guide for our style of life? If not, then what is our guide?

"Would you like to live in a commune? Why or why not? How would you parents feel if your teenage son or daughter joined a commune?

"Do the charges made against middle-class citizens and their high concern for possessing things trouble you? Is this closer to the truth than we'd like to admit?

"If you don't see the commune as a viable alternative to family life, what can we do to incorporate the values people find in communal living into our more traditional patterns?

"Now I hope we've given you enough material for discussion. As always, you may want to draw on some Biblical material that relates to this session."

Genesis 2:18–25
Luke 12:13–34; 18:18–30
Acts 2:44–47; 4:32–35

Chapter 12

New Roles for Women—and Men

"GOOD EVENING. We've come together tonight for the last session of our series on 'Men, Women, and God: Families Today and Tomorrow.' My impression from people's comments is that we've needed more time, but that some good things are already happening and more will happen, because all this won't just be forgotten. That's all we can ask for, I suspect.

"How will men and women relate to each other in the future? The feminist movement has made it clear that things are not going to be the same as they have been in the past. Women are insisting upon new roles and upon equal pay for equal work. They are also demanding, by implication, that the roles and status of men change, too. All of this will profoundly affect the family. I hope our presentations tonight will stimulate your thinking.

I

"For reasons that will quickly be clear, we've asked Dr. Ellen Parker to return tonight to be our first speaker."

"Thank you, Dr. Russell. I'm honored to have been asked to speak to you again.

"I am a career woman, 43 years old. I was married at nineteen and had a baby at twenty. My son died of pneumonia at the age of six months; the following year my husband and I were divorced.

"With help from my parents, I entered college. I am now a doctor in private practice, specializing in obstetrics and gynecology. I don't regret my choice. I have lived through a time when new doors of opportunity were opening everywhere for women. No longer are we confined to marriage or part-time positions by virtue of our sex. These doors, however, didn't open automatically. Pioneers had to push them open. I like to think that I've done a little bit of the pushing.

"A century ago higher education was rarely open to women; they had few opportunities to train for work other than household tasks and were economically dependent on the men of their families. Paul had set the tone centuries before when he said in 1 Corinthians 14:35, speaking of women, 'If there is anything they desire to know, let them ask their husbands at home. For it is shameful for a woman to speak in church.'

"I'd like to read a few lines from a book called *Decorum: A Practical Treatise on Etiquette and Dress of the Best American Society*, published in 1881. Among the bits of advice to gentlemen are: 'When addressing ladies, pay them the compliment of seeming to consider them capable of an equal understanding with gentlemen . . . they will appreciate the delicate compliment.' In another place the author says, 'Young married ladies must never appear in any public place unattended by their husbands or by elder ladies. This rule must never be infringed.'

"My response is to quote the cliché, 'You've come a long way, baby!' And we're still on the way. As recently as 1961, Supreme Court Justice Harlan, in ruling on a case concerning women's rights, said, 'Woman is regarded as the center of the home and family and therefore has her own special responsibilities.'

"Of course, there are differences between males and females, but a great deal of it is the result of social conditioning. For so long we have thought of certain forms of behavior as 'masculine' and some as 'feminine.' What do most people think of a boy who cuts out paper dolls? Or of a girl who plays football? Boys are not supposed to cry while girls are expected to be soft, sweet, and pretty.

"On the same subject of social conditioning Diana Trilling writes in *Saturday Review* in 1970 (10/10/70, p. 40, 'Female Biology in a Male Culture'):

. . . gone—or going . . . is the social-sexual differentiation between men and women in terms of dress and hairstyle. . . . the unisexual appearance of the sexes [is to be welcomed] if only for its criticism of a culture in which sexually differentiated styles of hair and dress, designed not by God but by man, were treated as if they were biological actualities. . . . whatever reduces the false separations between men and women is bound to reduce their suspicions and hostilities, and thus permit them a fuller expression of their human potentiality.

"The two sexes *are* different, but careful study of children and adults in all phases of their growth and achievement has forced a redefining of terms. Studies show that in rate of development, both physical and mental, the female leads. In muscular strength, the male is ahead, but the female has greater resistance to disease and death, and to emotional pressure. So how can you call either one 'the weaker sex'?

"Now that the revolution is finally being accomplished, I think relationships between men and women will be better all around. In my own field, once men were able to recognize that a woman colleague could be as good a doctor as a man, prejudice slowly melted and we were able to enjoy comradeship and cooperation. Medicine is a field in which your worth is established by your skill in dealing with clinical situations, and women doctors have now established their equal status. And of course no patient would dream of expecting to pay a lower fee to a woman doctor!

"Progress in certain other jobs and professions has come more slowly, and there are injustices yet to be removed. Among those that still hold out in defense of male supremacy, I'm afraid many churches are rather conspicuous. Maybe Dr. Russell will have something to say about that.

"So far I've talked about women. But of course the new climate is forcing men to change too. I said 'forcing' only because of male resistance to change. Really, I'd like to say that men as well as women are being liberated! In my opinion the traditional masculine roles have been hard on men. No doubt our primitive ancestors had to fight in order to survive; but in our modern world war is just silly and purposeless, as well as being horribly destructive. Our aggressive urges, if they have to be expressed, can be healthily used in overcoming barriers to human development, or in competitive sports. Evidence indicates that in these activities men have no significant superiority over women. Men have also been expected to work harder than women, and to assume greater burdens of responsibility. This has done them no good. On the contrary, it has reduced their average life-span to five or six years shorter than that of women. It just doesn't make sense—the work that has to be done and the responsibility that must be assumed can be equally shared by women and men.

"The sooner we get rid of our stereotypes the better. The weak, simpering woman who fainted at the sight of a mouse was a ridiculous Victorian fantasy. But so was the strong, masterful he-man, beating his hairy chest like a gorilla. So I see a much better future for both men and women. People are being liberated to work together in equal partnership—in the exciting task of building a better world for everyone to enjoy."

"Dr. Parker, I'm not happy about a few things you said. I'm a married woman and I'm not looking for any 'liberation,' as you call it! If there's resistance to change in this direction, you can count me in on the resistance, too! I don't think I'm the only woman, either! For instance, in our state legislature, when the Equal Rights Amendment was being discussed, are you aware of how many *women* opposed it? It was not only male resistance!

"I happen to like my way of life, and I don't feel like a second-class citizen. And I resent people continually telling me that's what I am!"

"I feel the same way!" comes a woman's voice from the other side of the room.

"Thank you—both of you. It's not fair for me to imply that *all* women seek liberation. But all of us will agree, I'm sure, that there are many women who feel trapped, manipulated, and degraded purely on the basis of sex. I agreed to come here today to speak out on their behalf."

"Thank you, Dr. Parker. As a pastor, I've enjoyed your presentation and the reaction you have stirred up. That's fine. We don't expect everyone to agree!

II

"Let's switch now from new roles of men and women outside the home to their new roles as family members. I'd like to present Florence Sinclair."

"Thank you, Dr. Russell. When my husband and I got married twelve years ago, we knew very little about the stirring changes Dr. Parker mentioned. Tom had finished college, with a degree in secondary education. I had completed my first year of college.

"With marriage I stopped my schooling. But that was all right—a lot of my friends did the same thing. I reasoned, who needs a degree in French to be a housewife?

"After four years and one baby, Tom wanted to return to school to work on his doctorate. The only way we could manage financially was if I went to work. I didn't mind doing that. Our baby was old enough for me to put her in a nursery.

"I found a job. The pay wasn't great, but the work was satisfying and within a year I had the first of several advancements. Tom studied hard, trying to complete his doctoral work as soon as possible. By careful budgeting, we lived on my salary.

"It's strange, but we never worked out the matter of family responsibilities. I continued doing everything around the house I had done before—plus working 42 hours a week. The only difference was that I had less time to do the work at home.

"One day I came to the end of my rope. It had been a particularly hard day at the office. I hadn't even taken a lunch break. I came home late, and as I rushed into our apartment, Tom kissed me on the cheek and asked, 'Hey, what's for supper, Flo?'

"That was too much! He had been studying all afternoon on the dining room table—a mere fifteen feet from the kitchen stove. Not a dish had been touched or an effort made toward helping. I had even picked Margie up from nursery school. I broke down and cried. I was angry and frustrated.

"We didn't have much of a supper that night. Tom opened a couple of cans and I heated up leftovers—but not before the two of us sat down and talked everything out.

"We suddenly realized that I had taken on two full-time jobs and he had only one! So we made a decision. We decided to divide up the work at home. It wasn't easy for either of us, and it's taken a long time for us to work out the details, but we're a team now. I have a career. I love my work—I'm an administrator of a public relations firm. I actually make more money than Tom does!

"We had our struggles in the beginning but Tom did one valuable thing: once we both realized I couldn't be a full-time worker and full-time housekeeper, he encouraged me. He kept saying that I ought to develop any talents I had. I'm so thankful for Tom. I think I'm a lucky woman to have an understanding husband who is willing to grow with me."

"I'm Tom Sinclair and I hadn't planned to say anything tonight, but as I've listened, I thought you might like to hear how I respond to what Flo has said.

"First of all, I never thought about the double load she was pulling. I'd never done much around the house, so I never thought about starting.

"Then Flo broke down one afternoon, like she said. We talked a long time. Oh, I agreed that we should both work at the house. But I kept thinking, what would the other guys say about it? Flo was great, though. Whenever I seemed to feel emasculated by this, she always had ways of proving to me that I was a great guy. That meant a lot.

"As I see it, I'm not just married to a mother and homemaker. I'm married to a woman who is a whole person. She's a lot more interesting than she was when we first married. Her life is as filled with excitement as mine is. We have so much to share with each other.

"Thanks for listening. I just wanted to add those words."

"Tom, I'm glad you spoke up. Now, I wonder if Florence has anything more to add."

"Yes, I'd like to speak a little more in generalities right now. I don't think we need to push sensational new patterns as much as flexibility that allows couples to arrange what suits them. This will mean challenging the sharp division of roles imposed on married couples in the past—for instance, the Germans used to say that the life of a woman was to be confined to 'Küche, Kinder, and Kirche' or kitchen, children, and church; anything outside that was none of their business.

"Flexibility won't always mean going as far as some married couples have gone, where wives have chosen to support the family, while husbands choose to do housework and care for the children.

"Flexibility seems good to me. I don't want women placed on a pedestal—and I don't want men up there either! I want no fixed roles for either of them, but freedom for each to be herself or himself. I believe families of the future will see the roles of the sexes as fluid and interchangeable. With the equal opportunities Dr. Parker mentioned, men and women will accept each other as comrades and equals."

"Thanks, Mrs. Sinclair, for sharing with us.

III

"Now it's my turn. I'd like to look at the family of the future from a Christian perspective. But first I'd like to point out that while many fingers point to the church as part of the problem in women's liberation, there is another side to that!

107

"For instance, there were women who traveled with Jesus and who helped support him and the twelve, according to Luke 8; and in Luke 23 we find that they even followed to Calvary. The point I make is that while there were no women among the twelve disciples, women weren't excluded either. They apparently were allowed to accompany Jesus in his travels, just as men were doing.

"We also need to think about the women Jesus talked to. What about the promiscuous woman at the well, in John 4? Jesus treated a woman everyone regarded as immoral with the same respect he would have shown to any other member of society. We could also talk about the woman taken in adultery or the woman who anointed his feet with oil and wiped them with her hair. Jesus didn't limit his respect to the wife of Herod's steward, who helped finance him; by his attitudes and acts, Jesus elevated the status of all women. And if I understand the feminists, what they're asking for is to be treated as equals with men. Jesus treated them that way.

"And Jesus' attitude was not without precedent in the Old Testament, even though like the New Testament it often reflects a basically male-dominated society. Women do emerge as leaders who command attention and are highly praised.

"For instance, the leadership of Deborah the female judge and champion of freedom is celebrated in Judges. We read later of a prophetess, Huldah, who exerted great influence at the time of King Josiah. My point is, while male dominance may have been the prevailing pattern of life, the Hebrews recognized the Spirit of God at work in women as well as in men. As the prophet Joel said, 'your sons and your *daughters* shall prophesy. . . . Even upon the menservants and *maidservants*, in those days, I will pour out my spirit.'

"In the New Testament, in addition to the attitude of Jesus, there are other bright spots. Philip the evangelist had four daughters who prophesied, or preached, and apparently they had some prominence in the church. Lydia, a well-known business-woman, cooperated with Paul in founding the church at Philippi. And we mustn't forget Priscilla, who had quite a remarkable ministry as a teacher and who often is mentioned before Aquila her husband when the two are referred to.

"In post-Biblical times, attitudes suggesting the inferiority of women persisted, and that's easily documented. But the ferment of Biblical insight continued to work in Christendom to bring about change. I suppose the classic statement of principle in this area is found in Paul's letter to the Galatians: 'There is neither Jew nor Greek, there is neither slave nor free, there is neither male nor female; for you are all one in Christ Jesus.' As I understand this verse, the apostle meant that when people become Christians, the human distinctions of sex, race, and social status are to be forgotten. We are now all one in Jesus Christ. This is a tremendous insight into God's will regarding the relationship of women and men.

"So while many people are still claiming the church is behind the times—and that's partially justifiable, I'm sure—the picture is not all bleak, and there has been progress. Here as in some other areas I wish the whole church had the vision of our international mission people. For a long time we have had women in greater numbers than men serving on foreign fields as leaders or as equal partners, even if it has only been recently that they have been ordained.

"But it does trouble me that the church has been so slow in accepting women as Jesus did. It also troubles me that Christians kept slaves, tortured heretics, encouraged wars, and tolerated injustice. Christians are human, imperfect instruments of God. But we're learning."

"Pastor, my name is Harriet Green. I've been sitting here listening to all this and I'd like to speak up. I'm not very calm about it, but I'd like to share some of the anguish I'm going through right now.

"I am a child of the church. I can't remember a time in my 29 years when I haven't been part of the church and the church has not been part of me. I could no more leave it than I could leave my soul.

"And yet, we are growing further and further apart. One of us is moving—me—and one of us us standing still—the church. Or at least the church is inching so slowly it appears unmoving. And what is coming between us is the issue of feminism. Or, more specifically, Christian feminism.

"For I am first a Christian, then a feminist. But if I didn't believe with all my heart that the goals of feminism are in line with my theological beliefs, then I would reject those goals. Yet what is the women's movement telling me but that I am someone of value? I have worth as a human being. And what has Jesus Christ told me but that he loved me enough to die for me, that *I was worth that much to him?*

"A friend gave me a button that proclaims, 'Jesus was a feminist.' I believe that. I believe not only that he is the great Liberator in the ultimate sense of freeing me from my sins, but also that through his actions and his message he has had a profound impact on the secular world. For Jesus did something that in his day was almost heretical—he treated women as people. Not as dogs, not as chattel, not as an afterthought, but as human beings equal to men. There is no place in the gospel where Jesus ever talks down to women, patronizes them, or pats them on the head and says, 'There, there, my words are beyond your understanding. Go ask your husband.' No! Not Jesus—not my Lord and Savior whom I worship and love.

"But let me tell you something. When I have tried to talk about being a Christian feminist in this church, that's what I get—a pat on the head, as though I am simply to be tolerated and then ignored. Or laughed at. Or else I get an angry 'You *can't* be a Christian and a feminist. That's a contradiction in terms. Read what Paul says in 1 Timothy and Ephesians and. . . .'

"And I say to you, with all due respect, that *Jesus* is my Lord, not Paul.

"Look, all I want from you—from the church—is to be *heard*—to be listened to with an open mind and an open heart. I want to explore the Scriptures as a whole with you—because we all know that to pick verses out of context is to risk perverting the Word of God. And I want to explore how the church can change to incorporate the talents and gifts of *all* its members. If we are truly brothers and sisters in Christ, then don't turn me away. Love me enough to listen to me."

"Harriet, thank you for saying that. Knowing you as I do, I'm sure that must have taken a lot of courage. I appreciate what you've said."

"But now it's time for our discussion groups.

IV

"Before you go, here are a few questions to consider. What does it mean that *both* woman and man are made in God's image (Genesis 1:27)? What does it really mean when we read in Galatians 3:28 that in Christ there is neither male nor female?

"How significant is it that Jesus was *male*? Wasn't his prime importance his humanness rather than his maleness? Could God have sent his only begotten *daughter*?

"Why did Jesus pick twelve male disciples? And when you discuss that, why did he pick twelve *Jews* and no Gentiles?

"I'd also like you to look carefully in your groups at 1 Timothy 2:8–15. This is the passage most commonly used against the ordination of women in the church. Look at the entire paragraph. If we deny leadership to women, mustn't we also deny them the right to braid their hair or to wear gold or pearls or expensive clothing? It's all in the same paragraph, remember.

"What about changing roles for males? Do men need liberation? Has the male of the species been as stereotyped and locked in as the female?

"What would our church look like if women had an equal voice with men? Whether you realize it or not, we have 54% female members in our congregation but only two women on our board. What would it feel like for you men if the situation were reversed and the board had only 12½% men?

"I think we've given you some questions to discuss in your small groups. In addition to the Bible passages I just referred to, some others are listed that were mentioned tonight."

Genesis 1:27
Judges 4–5
2 Kings 22:11–20
Joel 2:28–29
Luke 7:36–50; 8:1–3; 23:55–24:11
John 8:2–11
Acts 16:1–40; 18:2, 18, 26; 21:9
Romans 16:3
Galatians 3:28
1 Timothy 2:8–15
2 Timothy 4:19